ON THE
SUNNY SIDE
OF THE
STREET

ON THE SUNNY SIDE OF THE STREET

*The Life and Lyrics
of Dorothy Fields*

DEBORAH GRACE WINER

Foreword by Betty Comden

Schirmer Books
An Imprint of Simon & Schuster Macmillan
New York

Prentice Hall International
London Mexico City New Delhi Singapore Sydney Toronto

Credits and permissions can be found on pp. 265–267 and should be considered an extension of the copyright page.

Copyright © 1997 by Deborah Grace Winer

Schirmer Books
An Imprint of Simon & Schuster Macmillan
1633 Broadway
New York, New York 10019

Library of Congress Catalog Card Number: 97-11998

Printed in the United States of America

Printing Number

1 2 3 4 5 6 7 8 9 10

Library of Congress Cataloging-in-Publication Data

Winer, Deborah Grace.
    On the sunny side of the street : the life and lyrics of Dorothy
Fields / Deborah Grace Winer.
    p.   cm.
    Includes index.
    ISBN 0-02-864730-0 (alk. paper)
    1. Fields, Dorothy, 1905-1974. 2. Lyricists—United States—
Biography. 3. Librettists—United States—Biography. 4. Popular
music—United States—Texts. I. Fields, Dorothy, 1905-1974.
Lyrics. Selections. II. Title.
ML423.F4W56   1998
782.42164'092—dc21
        [B]   97-11998
                                                                  CIP
                                                                   MN

This paper meets the requirements of ANSI/NISO Z.39.48-1992 (Permanence of Paper).

TO MY FAMILY, AND TO ALL THOSE
WHO KEEP THESE SONGS ALIVE.

CONTENTS

FOREWORD

A S A LITTLE KID I KNEW LOTS OF POPULAR
songs. I heard them on the radio, people whistled them
on the streets, friends had the sheet music propped up on
their pianos, my young aunt who lived with us sang them while
helping out with the dishes. She was a Berlin expert, but she also
sang, over and over, "I Can't Give You Anything but Love, Baby."
And I loved it. I didn't know who wrote it. We didn't seem to know
who wrote the songs. They were just there . . . in the air . . . part of
the fabric of our lives. That must be the first Dorothy Fields lyric I
ever knew.

When in the mid-1940s I did my first show on Broadway, *On
the Town,* with Adolph Green and Leonard Bernstein, there were
almost no women writing for the musical theatre. But Dorothy, who
was about to do *Annie Get Your Gun,* had already been a star lyricist for two decades.

She was *the* woman songwriter. But woman or man, it made
no difference either in her work or in the esteem in which she was
held by her colleagues. She was a superb lyricist with enormous
range: from "Sunny Side of the Street" to "The Way You Look
Tonight" to "Big Spender"—collaborating with composers as different from one another as Jimmy McHugh, Jerome Kern, and Cy
Coleman. The marvelous thing about the way Dorothy wrote is that
her lyrics were inventive without being tricky. She didn't engage in
clever wordplay just for its own sake. She could do it—but she
never compromised her direct, fresh manner of expressing a
thought.

I knew Dorothy mainly in the latter part of her life. I always
thought she was a wonderful looking woman, very chic, great eyes,
a beautiful manner. And she was bright and funny, and famous for
giving great parties. The fact that even as she got older she was
able to stay in tune with the younger generation was one of the
remarkable things about her, and enabled her in later years to produce work as authentically contemporary as *Sweet Charity*.

FOREWORD

I cheer this book celebrating Dorothy Fields's contributions to American music and the musical theatre. In *On the Sunny Side of the Street* Deborah Grace Winer gives us a marvelous picture of a remarkable woman and the times in which she lived and created her songs, so many of which have achieved great distinction and become part of our everyday American life.

—Betty Comden

PREFACE

AS A TEENAGE OLD-MOVIE ADDICT, I became a fan of Dorothy Fields the moment I heard Fred Astaire sing "I Won't Dance" to Ginger Rogers. Anyone who could write "For heaven rest us / I'm not asbestos," I decided, had to be blessed. The ensuing years only confirmed that hunch, particularly when I realized that she did it all as the lone female amid the old-boy club of legends that gave us the American songbook.

Dorothy Fields's career is the story of Broadway, Hollywood, and popular music for the better part of the twentieth century. This book is intended as a portrait and a chronicle, to try and put the woman and her work in perspective. The selection of lyrics I've included is not meant to be exhaustive, but, rather, representative of the span of her talents, and they include her most well-known contributions, from the song from which the book takes its title to "Big Spender."

Perhaps most gratifying in the several years since I began this project has been the enthusiastic reaction to such a venture from the music and theatre community. I received an enormous amount of support from the Fields family, from Dorothy's friends and colleagues (and colleagues' children), and from musical theatre experts and icons, as well as from other journalists.

First, I'm grateful to Dorothy Fields's children, Eliza Lahm Brewster and particularly David Lahm, who extended himself in every way possible, not only to provide me with as many candid and sensitive insights into his mother's life as I sought, but who always made an effort to put me in touch with others, answer questions, ease the official wheels, and generally help out in an ever-gracious manner. The permissions granted me regarding the use of lyrics are central to the book's scope, and the powers in both the Fields estate and the interests of her collaborators were tremendously cooperative, beginning with Albert DaSilva, who runs the Fields camp (along with Cy Coleman's and Sigmund Romberg's) and who couldn't have been nicer or more helpful. Lucille Meyers of the Jimmy McHugh estate was of kind and valuable aid, as was Ken Strnad of the Songwriters Guild of America; on behalf of the Jerome Kern estate, R. Andrew Boose gave me every consideration; also Frank Military and Jack Rosner of Warner-Chappell Music.

I also must thank Cy Coleman, Albert Hague, and Burton and Lynn Lane for their cooperation. Burton Lane, who was one of these only three surviving collaborators, passed away a few weeks after our meeting for this book, and his thoughts on Dorothy mark his final interview. Many people gave freely of their time to talk with me. Special thanks to Mary Ellin (Berlin) Barrett, Jerome and Rhea Chodorov, Jamie Hammerstein, Fred Ebb, Lucie Arnaz, Sheldon Harnick, Mary Rodgers, Jonathan Schwartz, Michael Feinstein, Ruth Mitchell, Becky Stein, Frank Wiener, Dr. Molly Harrower, and Alexandra Mayes Birnbaum. Also, Miles Kreuger and his Institute of the American Musical, Bert Fink of the Rodgers and Hammerstein Organization, Michael Kerker of ASCAP, Sam Gill, Warren Sherk, Robert Cushman, and particularly Faye Thompson of the Academy of Motion Picture Arts and Sciences Margaret Herrick Library and Film Archive, the staff of the Billy Rose Theatre Collection at the New York Public Library, Lincoln Center, the Columbia University Oral History Project, and the 92nd Street Y's Lyrics and Lyricists series. Heartfelt thanks to Marc and Armond Fields, whose book *From the Bowery to Broadway: Lew Fields and the Roots of American Popular Theater* was a valuable source on the early years, as were the several unpublished interviews they shared with me. For their personal help or the insight their work lent as sources, thanks to Hugh Fordin, Lee Davis, Steven Suskin, Philip Furia, Max Wilk, Patricia Bosworth, Gerald Bordman, Rex Reed, Stanley Green, Martin Gottfried, Roger Lax, and Dwight Blocker Bowers.

Thanks as well to Rosemary Clooney for her support in my Los Angeles exploits, to Ken Bloom for his song list, to Mary Cleere Haran, who was forever sharing her research, enthusiasm, and general moral support, to Toba Brill Winer and Ita Pasztor, and to Jessica Daryl Winer for her research assistance.

Jonathan Wiener, my editor at Schirmer Books, championed this from the beginning and lent the project his unending patience and expertise. My appreciation goes as well to others at the publisher who made this possible, particularly production editor Jane Andrassi; also Paul Boger, Richard Carlin, and Lisa Chovnick.

Special thanks to my agent, Tom Wallace; and for providing the book with a foreword, sincerest gratitude to another lion of the musical theatre, Betty Comden.

INTRODUCTION

A T THE END OF THE DECADE that had transformed America's mass music into rock and roll, the
National Academy of Popular Music established the
Songwriters Hall of Fame to honor the architects of the music that
had for most of the twentieth century pervaded and anchored the
country's popular culture. At a cocktail reception and dinner in
1971, ten giants of American song were inducted as charter members—joining Irving Berlin and Richard Rodgers the list included
Harold Arlen, Duke Ellington, Ira Gershwin, Johnny Mercer—all
of them men, with the exception of one.

As the only major-league woman songwriter of the golden age
of American popular song and musical theatre, Dorothy Fields had
been standing virtually alone among men for almost fifty years,
since first beginning her career in the 1920s, writing lyrics for
Harlem's Cotton Club revues. Teamed with over a dozen of the
American songbook's most prominent composers (beginning with
Jimmy McHugh), she is responsible for hits that are ingrained in
American culture: "On the Sunny Side of the Street," "I Can't Give
You Anything but Love," "I'm in the Mood for Love," "A Fine
Romance," "The Way You Look Tonight," "Lovely to Look At,"
"Pick Yourself Up," "I Won't Dance," "Don't Blame Me," "I Feel a
Song Comin' On," "I Must Have That Man," "Exactly Like You,"
"Close as Pages in a Book," "You Couldn't Be Cuter," "Bojangles of
Harlem," "Make the Man Love Me," "Big Spender," "If My Friends
Could See Me Now"—altogether, some 400 songs penned in her
lifetime. She provided lyrics and/or librettos for such Broadway
shows as *Sweet Charity*, *Seesaw*, *Mexican Hayride*, *A Tree Grows in
Brooklyn*, *Redhead*, *Up in Central Park*, and *Annie Get Your Gun*,
which was born at her inspiration. She wrote lyrics for more than
thirty films, including the Fred Astaire-Ginger Rogers stalwarts
Roberta and *Swing Time*.

Success came early to her, and was fairly constant for decades.
She began working with Jerome Kern after RKO assigned her to
write lyrics for a sixteen-bar melody of his that became "Lovely to

Look At." By the next year, and two movies later, the song "The Way You Look Tonight" won Kern and his thirty-year-old lyricist an Academy Award. Yet Dorothy Fields never enjoyed the same kind of name recognition among the general public as did her collaborators Jerome Kern, Jimmy McHugh, Harold Arlen, Sigmund Romberg, Arthur Schwartz, Harry Warren, Burton Lane, and Cy Coleman; her colleagues Richard Rodgers, Irving Berlin, and Hoagy Carmichael; and her fellow lyricists Larry Hart, Ira Gershwin, Johnny Mercer, and Oscar Hammerstein II. Certainly, her personal fame outside the entertainment community never came close to being commensurate with the renown of the standards she produced. Up until her death in 1974, she often encountered people who would suddenly exclaim in realization, "*You* wrote *that*?"—a situation that, publicly, anyway, she'd always joke about.

Tall, with dark hair and eyes and a slim, Sunday-tennis-player appearance that throughout her life remained a beacon of impeccable grooming and taste, Dorothy Fields represented the sophisticated, urbane wit that epitomized New York creative circles in the Jazz Age. But rather than the acid cynicism of, for instance, that other Dorothy—the legendary Miss Parker, who fed the Algonquin Round Table with light verse bemoaning the inconvenience of suicide methods—Dorothy Fields combined her unsentimental jazz-age hip with a romantic optimism.

After all, it wasn't the rarefied literary set in which she came of age, but in the commercial theatre and Tin Pan Alley. There, Ira Gershwin and Larry Hart were already busy winning over the paying public with a fresh new voice: a slangy sophistication—literary, but that also stuck a pin in the ardent poetry of the operetta-style musicals that had dominated until recently. Their protagonists weren't slobbering undying passion. Never mind "I love you." Gershwin read that as "You're a Builder Upper." Hart's idea of romance was to "go to Coney and eat baloney . . . ." For the young Dorothy Fields, devotion meant the promise of "diamond bracelets Woolworth doesn't sell."

Dorothy came naturally to the theatre, minus the leap into show business that would have faced other young ladies of the period. The reason was that she was born into a theatrical dynasty, the daughter of vaudeville star/manager/producer Lew Fields. Lew was half of Weber and Fields, who convulsed turn-of-the-century audiences with their ethnic "Dutchman" comedy, and who are credited with originating the custard pie in the face and the joke that begins, "Who was that lady I saw you with last night?" (The answer, of course, being "That was no lady, that was my wife.") Later, as a producer, Lew Fields became a showman-predecessor to Florenz Ziegfeld and widely influenced musical comedy in the early twentieth century. Between 1896 and 1927, six Broadway theatres bore Fields's name, and among his discoveries were Rodgers and Hart, whose early shows he produced.

Stardom aside, the theatrical profession was still disreputable enough for Lew to want to keep his family away from it. Nevertheless, three of his four children would end up there. Dorothy and her two brothers would, as writers, eventually dominate Broadway in the 1940s: Herbert, as a librettist, teamed with Dorothy on such shows *Annie Get Your Gun*, and also, from the '20s, authored all the early Rodgers and Hart books and collaborated with Cole Porter and Vincent Youmans on the smashes *Panama Hattie* and *Hit the Deck*; and oldest brother, Joseph, the playwright responsible for a string of hits including *My Sister Eileen* (with Jerome Chodorov) and *Gentlemen Prefer Blondes* (with Anita Loos).

Dorothy, who came of age in the flapper era, was a direct product of the freedom women had won for themselves in rebelling against Victorian ideas of where they belonged. Chaste, idealized womanhood was out, liberated "moderns" were in—active participants in the world around them, meeting men on their own turf, be it speakeasies or sex. On the other hand, outside of a couple of cities like New York and Chicago, the country wasn't anywhere near ready for that, particularly after the stock market crashed and the country went into the Depression. The idea that women should be assertive—and worse, admit that sex held a few charms beyond wifely duty—was downright alarming.

Here was Dorothy Fields, in 1936, writing, "I've never mussed the crease in your blue serge pants" in a song ("A Fine Romance") that is a series of complaints about a lover "as cold as yesterday's mashed potatoes." Dorothy's lyrics, apart from their wit, were sensual, suggestive, appreciative of sex—though no more risqué than those of contemporaries like Hart, Porter, or Gershwin; the only difference was that the sentiments were being expressed by a woman. Certainly, the first half of the twentieth century held a complement of women writers and poets who wore sensuality on their sleeve—and naturally led the requisite lives of bohemian debauchery, or even worse, European bohemian debauchery.

But in an age when women never broke through the confines of home, family, and society's dictates of "appropriateness," Dorothy was a hybrid, independent as a professional in a man's field, given credence at the same time by her "respectability"— attractive, feminine, wife and mother—her views not dismissable as "demimonde morals."

Perhaps one of the greatest explanations for Dorothy Fields's mainstream acceptance was that she was mainstream. A pioneer— absolutely. Conventional in lifestyle and her embrace of the establishment—positively. She was never a youthful rebel, rather one of the successful Broadway party crowd. She wasn't a communist, she was a Republican. She didn't toil through the night caught up with the divine muse, she began work punctually every morning at eight o'clock with a yellow pad and pencil. Though she enjoyed the company of men, she didn't flaunt affairs and shack up with composers or bullfighters; she was married once to a doctor, and when that failed, to a businessman, to whom she stayed married some twenty years, until his death, having two children and a house in Brewster, New York; and newspapers didn't report her wild escapades, but her charity work with the Girl Scouts of America.

It was not a life without trials and problems, especially in her later years. But they were the kind of difficulties common to many households. To the show business establishment (which, after all, she'd been born into) and to the public, Dorothy Fields didn't threaten—she struck a universal chord with her life-embracing wit and uniquely feminine perspective.

If Dorothy Fields wasn't the only woman songwriter in America's pre-rock and roll music scene (and there were a number of others), she was the only one to achieve an equal stature among the top echelon male writers who drove pop and show music, to be "one of the club," both in magnitude and consistency of hits, and in producing a body of significant, mainstream work spanning many decades. Aside from star singers like Billie Holiday or Peggy Lee, who wrote a number of songs they then recorded, Dorothy is the only female songwriter of the golden age whose name has not sunk into oblivion with time. ASCAP, in fact, continues to assign her work the highest performance rating of any woman on its rolls.

It's Dorothy who paved the way for successors like Betty Comden, Carolyn Leigh, and Marilyn Bergman and eventually, the generation of feminist folk/rock bards that would include Carole King, Joni Mitchell, Judy Collins, and Carly Simon.

Ironically, Dorothy Fields has the distinction of being the only composer or lyricist of the American songbook to successfully span a career of six decades, to stay viable from the 1920s, with hits all the way into the 1970s. The most formidable giants of the business either didn't live to accomplish that, or more often, hit a point after the arrival of rock and roll where their careers simply waned. Even Richard Rodgers, bedrock of the American musical, who continued to write well after the death of Hammerstein, had a series of failures beginning in the mid-'60s, like *Do I Hear a Waltz?* and *Two by Two*, from which his career never recovered. Dorothy's answer to the '60s was *Sweet Charity*, with a new collaborator, Cy Coleman, who was some twenty-five years younger than her sixty. *Seesaw*, again with Coleman, would follow in the early '70s, yielding the songs "Nobody Does It Like Me," and appropriately, "It's Not Where You Start, It's Where You Finish."

The fact that her lyrics stayed so genuinely contemporary is also a large part of her longevity. Her trademark true ear for slangy phrasing (never embarrassed or pandering) makes her lyrics for Coleman's rock-scented *Sweet Charity* score as fresh as the 1930 "On the Sunny Side of the Street" still sounds today. The years since her death have brought her more recognition not only as a pillar of the American songbook and a feminist pioneer, but as a "lyricist's lyricist," prompting *New Yorker* jazz and pop critic Whitney Balliett to write, "Not until Sondheim did anyone rival her interior rhymes." In 1996 the U.S. Postal Service issued a Dorothy Fields stamp as part of a block of four songwriter stamps that also included Harold Arlen, Hoagy Carmichael, and Johnny Mercer.

The story of Dorothy Fields goes beyond a tribute to one woman's talent and craft. Her life and times are a chronicle of the golden age of Broadway, Hollywood, and Tin Pan Alley, and the ways in which America transformed itself from the Jazz Age to the Age of Aquarius.

ON THE
SUNNY SIDE
OF THE
STREET

"You have to be more polite than other children, because your father is an actor."

—Rose Fields

DOROTHY FIELDS was born on July 15, 1905—not in New York City, where her family lived, but in the seaside town of Allenhurst, New Jersey. The story goes like this: Lew Fields and his wife, Rose, were enjoying the beach across from their rented summer home on the Jersey shore, when Rose went into labor. Lew and their weekend guests, Lee Shubert, of the theatre-owning Shubert brothers, and Willie Collier, the vaudeville comedian and actor, rushed Rose back to the house, and Collier went off in search of the doctor. Unable to find him, he returned instead with the woman who ran the newsstand at the corner, who was also a midwife. And thus Dorothy Fields was brought into the world.

Lew and Rose had been parents three times before; the family already consisted of eleven-year-old Frances, ten-year-old Joseph, and Herbert, age six. Notwithstanding summer at the shore, the Fieldses' usual life revolved around their townhouse off Riverside Drive on the Upper West Side of Manhattan. The affluent neighborhood was often referred to as "the gilded ghetto," because of its well-heeled, predominantly Jewish residents who lived lives of successful solidity as lawyers, Wall Street brokers, doctors, and respectable businessmen. A few blocks down West End Avenue, Dr. William Rodgers maintained an office and apartment where his younger son, Dick, practiced the piano.

Lew Fields, in the early part of the century, had been one of the most successful—and certainly one of the busiest—men on Broadway, performing, managing and touring vaudeville and musical comedy, and producing new shows each season. Always aware of appearances and establishing the foundations of respectability (the

Lew Fields, dressed for the office

last thing the rest of the world associated with show business, of which he was all too painfully conscious), he lived lavishly, though never flashily, like his neighbors. Rose Fields presided over a household that included a cook, a maid, a chauffeur-handyman, a governess to look after the children, and a laundress who came in several days a week. There was, as well, a summer home.

This was a far cry from Lew's origins in the slums of the Lower East Side. He'd been one of a family of four brothers, the sons of Solomon and Sarah Schoenfeld, who came over to America in 1872 from an area of Poland nearer to Germany than to its Russian captors. Actually, Lew (who was then known as Moses) was five years old when his family immigrated; in his lifetime, while making no bones about his upbringing on the Bowery, he never acknowledged the fact that he hadn't been born in the United States.

Tenement living in the neighborhoods surrounding the Bowery in those days was cramped, without adequate sewage, waste disposal, refrigeration, or ventilation, a magnet for vermin, fire, and disease. The dirt streets were clogged with vendors and refuse and crowds. Gangs of youths from the different ethnic groups who lived there would regularly get into street fights if territories were invaded. Up until the arrival of the Jews who came over around the time of the Schoenfelds, the last influx into the neighborhood had been the Irish, and before them, the Germans, who were beginning to graduate out. The Italians would come later, along with a second, larger arrival of European Jews from farther east.

Solomon Schoenfeld was a tailor by trade, and in the tiny tenement apartment he set up a sweatshop, where everyone in the household worked cutting, sewing, pressing, and delivering the piece goods that allowed them barely to scrape by. The family took on the name of Schanfield (later dropping the c) and the boys adopted more "American" first names—Max, Sol, Lewis, and Charles—as part of the public school-teachers' crusade for "simplification." It was attending the Henry Street School that Lew first met Joe Weber, also from a family of immigrants, and they became fast friends. Their antics when the teachers' backs were turned, like doing back flips to amuse their classmates, eventually got them expelled.

At the age of twelve, the two got themselves their first professional job at one of the myriad dime museums that populated the Bowery, which offered their patrons an assortment of thrills ranging from freaks to curiosities with "scientific" trappings to variety acts, some grotesque or lewd, some suitable for women and families, depending on the venue. Morris and Hickman's East Side Museum was a "clean" museum (no gambling or prostitution) and in the basement (below the floors that held the Chinese Giant, the Turtle Boy, the Glass Eater, and the stuffed rat that was supposedly the one trained in prison by President Garfield's assassin), the boys did an Irish act in which, dressed in green vests, derbies, and canes, they sang, danced, and did "knockabout" comedy—basically every rough and tumble stunt, pratfall, and assault on each other that they could think of to amuse their cheering, howling, beer-loving audience. From the start they were a hit, and began doing ten turns a day for the then princely sum of three dollars a week each.

Weber and Fields (Lew had streamlined his name once more; the rest of his family would follow) quickly moved on to greater vaudeville success, developing the "Mike and Meyer" routines with their "Dutch" humor. (Actually Holland was not any more involved than it is in "Pennsylvania Dutch"; in both cases "Dutch" stands for deutsch—"German.") As Mike, Joe Weber padded his girth. Lew was the tall, thin Meyer, who was interminably trying to part Mike from his money through various schemes. They delivered their banter in a German-Jewish dialect that butchered the language with malapropisms and logic foreshadowing Abbott and Costello's "Who's on First?" And they refined their strenuous physical slapstick into increasingly evolved and orchestrated routines, like their famous "choking routine."

In the age of political correctness and ethnic sensitivity, it's hard to think back to a time when an entire act could be based on dialect and stereotyping. Then again, blackface was also at the height of its appeal. But there is truth in the cliché that "these were different times," when New York and other urban centers were teeming with newcomers completely alien to one another and to the society that was absorbing them. Close quarters and the "in-your-face" ethnicity of these communities, which were nevertheless heading for assimilation together, made it natural for comedians of different stripes to laugh at themselves and their neighbors. Though on the streets young toughs would protect their Irish, Jewish, or Italian gang's territory from the others, in the theatres, the humor only seemed to soften the barriers and make more familiar that

THE THEATRE

Father Lew and daughter Dorothy,
when she was about three

which was foreign. And audiences did laugh. Soon the young comedy team was engaged by impresario Oscar Hammerstein I for his Olympia Theatre and playing at Tony Pastor's, which had the distinction of raising vaudeville to a quality and respectability of entertainment as suitable for the family as any legitimate theatre. (It had a $1.50 top ticket price, the same as for a legit house.)

It was while he and Joe Weber were working at Tony Pastor's that Lew met Rose (then Harris), who was a Brooklyn friend of his little sister's. They were married in 1893. Touring the circuits of the Northeast and Midwest increased Joe and Lew's renown until they were among the most famous duos on the boards. They began putting together their own companies of variety acts, which became generally known as the Weberfields, playing both in New York and on the road. Over the next several decades, with and without Joe Weber, Lew would produce a stream of variety shows and travesties of serious legitimate hits (David Belasco's plays were a favorite target), often in partnership with the Shubert brothers, Lee and J. J., and in which he often performed himself. The shows that emanated from the Weber and Fields Music Hall (with titles like *Fiddle-dee-dee*, *Hoity-Toity*, and *Quo Vass Iss*) in turn set a new standard for "clean" music hall entertainment. The companies included such stars as Lillian Russell, Fay Templeton, David Warfield, William Collier, and Marie Dressler. (Among the performers Lew discovered were Vernon Castle and Helen Hayes.) The line of chorus girls at the Music Hall was known to be exceptional, and unlike elsewhere, they were treated with the same respect as the stars. Lew went solo in 1904, the year before Dorothy was born, after tensions had increased with Joe Weber. (They would reunite on and off, in business and for performing.) He opened the Lew Fields Theatre on West 42nd Street, designed and built by Oscar Hammerstein I, and went on to a producing and performing career that would rival that of another powerhouse, his contemporary George M. Cohan. (There was, in fact, a song made popular by Weberfields star John T. Kelly called "If It Wasn't for the Irish and the Jews," with one verse: "I really heard Belasco say / You couldn't stage a play today / If it wasn't . . . .")

If Lew was consumed with the theatre, actively involved with every aspect of production, he was a completely different man at home. There, Rose ran things with a grip of iron, while Lew was content to be passive and even withdrawn. In what was clearly a matriarchal setup, to the end of her life Rose was referred to as "the Queen." The Fieldses were an affectionate family—the father would kiss the boys, and they each other, and Lew's reputation offstage as

Lew Fields, Frances Fields looking chic, and Lew's discovery, a young Helen Hayes

a kind, genial, though serious man was not lost on his household, except that he was prone to moodiness and sudden, unprovoked bursts of temper, from which Rose tried to protect the children.

That is, when he was home at all. In truth, his immersion in his work was so complete, his schedule of rehearsing, producing, performing, and touring so breakneck, that he was practically unknown to his children. One story has a two-year-old Dorothy

Dorothy as a young teen, at the beach

running crying and screaming from the room when her father, still in costume, had rushed home for a quick dinner with his kids between shows; she didn't know who the stranger was.

That episode aside, the children idolized him, especially the younger ones. Dorothy grew into a very self-possessed child, a real Daddy's girl, and from the age of around seven, she was the designated keeper of her father's scrapbooks. Rose, on the other hand, did everything she could to isolate the family from her husband's professional world, terrified that one day they would take it up themselves. Lew also felt that way; he always dressed more like a businessman than a theatrical "sport," and behaved according to the level of gentility of the patrons he wanted to attract. (To the end, Lew remained an immaculate dresser, never without a pointed handkerchief in his breast pocket.) They rarely entertained a lot of theatre folk at home.

Still, Dorothy and Herb, especially, relished the occasions when they were allowed to go to their father's theatre and stand in the wings, or sit out front and watch him work. At a Saturday or Sunday matinee, Dorothy would march backstage and fearlessly go up to whatever performers were around and say, "I'm Lew Fields's daughter," and she was the instant center of attention, fussed over with "Oh, I'm so glad to meet you, what's your name?" She would sit in the audience, and family pal "Uncle" Willie Collier, doing some onstage business with scrambled eggs, would, in front of the whole audience, offer some to her.

When Lew and Joe Weber reunited for their 1912 Jubilee, the whole family went out on a coast-to-coast tour, with their own private railroad car on a train that had "Weber and Fields Jubilee" in letters along the outside. It was really the first time the Fields children had seen their father work as a performer, and it only made them idolize him even more. When Lillian Russell got married in Pittsburgh to businessman and later ambassador Alexander Moore, Dorothy was a flower girl, and Willie Collier's son, Buster, was an usher. Russell, whose name had been Helen Leonard until Tony Pastor changed it around the time his music hall launched her as the quintessential star of the Gilded Age,

TEN CENTS

THE

DEVOTED EXCLUSIVELY TO THE · PROFESSION OF ENTERTAINMENT

SHOW WORLD

WARREN A. PATRICK · · GENERAL DIRECTOR.

Vol. III No. 13 · CHICAGO · September

LEW FIELDS

AND

THE GIRL BEHIND THE COUN

LEW FIELDS.

CONNIE EDDIS

LEW FIELDS AND HIS PLAYERS.

was curvy, sexy, to be reckoned with both as a singer and comedienne, a magnet for husbands (her own and other people's), and a high roller at the gaming tables.

When seven-year-old Dorothy and little Buster were romping around the train one day on tour, they happened on Russell's open stateroom. Dorothy later recalled that Russell had the most beautiful collection of wigs, and apparently for good reason; when Buster and Dorothy looked through the inadvertently opened door they found her to be bald: "Not a spear of hair on her head," Dorothy remembered. The children screamed, and were immediately sworn to silence.

Lillian Russell wasn't the only gambler in the group. In fact, gambling was Lew's greatest weakness, and was the reason that despite the lavish lifestyle he projected to the world, he was constantly on the brink of financial ruin. He frequented "gentlemen's clubs" like Canfield's and Daly's, and was fond of the track. When zealous district attorney William Travers Jerome began a crackdown on gambling in New York, he organized a series of raids on the tony clubs around town. Jesse Lewisohn, Lillian Russell's companion and a friend of Lew's, was arrested in 1902 while at the races with Russell for refusing to cooperate with a subpoena. Lew escaped direct attack, but was frequently mentioned in the papers being spotted at the track or more indoor establishments. Rose, who lived to keep any kind of publicity from tainting the family name, left him twice over his problem, once, Dorothy remembered, packing up the children in Saratoga and returning to the city.

Lew tried to be more discreet, but the enormous pressures and precariousness of his financial situation only became worse over the years. In the already tenuous world of the theatre, he was trying to produce hits and tour them, surviving the flops, owing money to everybody both in business and for personal debts, often being forced to perform himself for the audience his presence would bring in, and driving himself to exhaustion keeping the real situation from Rose and the rest of the family.

Left page: Impresario Fields and his company of talent

The family had moved into a larger house on West 90th Street, around the time that Lew and Rose took in Rose's orphaned teenage nephew, Herb Harris (who was about the same age as their son Joe), to raise as their own, bringing even more financial pressure. Eventually, Lew would collapse with a breakdown, but despite the doctors' instructions, he would cut short the prescribed vacation, declare himself "a new man," and dive right back into his schedule. The financial strains never took a permanent turn for the better, and in some years led to a frantic brush with bankruptcy that left Lew pleading with the Shuberts for help. Scaling down their lifestyle in terms of the number of servants and moving finally to an apartment on West End Avenue only solved part of the problem.

It was ultimately Frances's new husband, Charles Marcus, who bailed out his in-laws. Frances, eleven years older than Dorothy and a debutante, had married into a successful banking family, in what Joe, Herb, and Dorothy always referred to as "the merger." Frances was sweet, placid, and so sheltered in her upbringing (even more so, as the eldest girl, than the other children) as to be somewhat unworldly. For her, husband, home, and family were what mattered. The other three Fields children were another breed. Joe was a burly youth, who inherited his father's wry deadpan. He played football and the plan was for him to pursue a career in law. His gifts, however, were in writing and painting, which he enjoyed; however, unlike his younger siblings, he would get a late start in their father's profession because he went off to Europe (after college), and then he and his cousin Herb Harris, from whom he'd been inseparable since Harris joined the family, went into the perfume business together.

Herb Fields, who was four years younger than Joe, couldn't have been more different. He was slight and sensitive, with a quick wit and a love of the stage, dance, music, costumes—anything to do in any way with the theatre. From childhood, he came up with verse and rhymes that led Lew to joke about having a librettist in the family—something that would turn out to be true, and would eventually give the old man a new lease on his career. Herb worshiped his father, was awed by him, and was forever trying to win his approval.

Dorothy was six years Herb's junior. Straightforward, bright, with a quiet and wicked verbal wit, she took in everything around her with the perceptiveness that would serve her so well as a lyricist. She was active and athletic and anything she got into, she did well. Then, as later on, she loved to play tennis, and there were new courts right around the corner from their home, where her father had also avidly taken up the sport. Dorothy, like her sister, Frances, was brought up very much as a young lady. She attended the Benjamin School for Girls, a finishing school on Manhattan's Upper West Side, where she was on the basketball team with Hal Prince's mother. Another school chum would years later become the second Mrs. Joe Fields. At school, Dorothy won prizes in basketball, English (for poetry), and dramatics.

One sweltering summer Sunday in 1919 a young composer named Dick Rodgers arrived at the Fieldses' summer home in Far

Dorothy in flapper days

Rockaway. He'd been sent by a mutual friend, Phil Leavitt, the son of the family who rented the house next door. About to enter the freshman class at Columbia University, Rodgers had taken the train out from the city to play for the great Lew Fields some of the songs he'd been writing with his new partner, Larry Hart (Leavitt had brought the two of them together as well). Hart had begged off the trip, claiming a headache. (Rodgers recalled that he always did that whenever selling themselves was involved.) When he arrived, the whole family was waiting, and Rose and Lew, along with the four younger Fieldses, tried to make their nervous visitor (who'd been expecting an audience of one) comfortable. Rodgers was immediately smitten with fourteen-year-old Dorothy, whom he described as having "the most dazzling eyes" he'd ever seen, and he spent the rest of the afternoon trying harder to impress her than her father.

Lew was so won over by what he heard that he bought one of the unpublished duo's songs on the spot. The song was "Any Old Place with You," a catchy travel song (lyrics a lot like Ira Gershwin and Yip Harburg's later "Let's Take a Walk Around the Block") that showcased Larry Hart's budding virtuousity, rhyming "Portugal" with "court you, gal," and the big finish, "I'd go to hell for ya / Or Philadelphia." Not only did Lew buy it, he interpolated it into the current show on Broadway he was producing and starring in, *A Lonely Romeo.*

The friendship that ensued between Rodgers and Hart and the Fields family would help change the face of American musical comedy over the next decade. It would also provide the nucleus of a youthful and energetic social group that would enter the profession by way of amateur shows. Herb Fields was also at Columbia, until Lew's financial problems forced him to leave, and soon hooked up with the pixieish, erratic, and tormented Larry, and Dick, whose solid manner seemed more suited to a businessman, and the three began to collaborate. First, there was a commission from the Akron Club, a social-athletic club of which Dick's older brother, Morty, was a member. The show was called *You'd Be Surprised*, and was to benefit camp vacations for poor children, and it ran for one night— March 6, 1920—in the Grand Ballroom of the Plaza Hotel. Lew Fields was credited with "Professional Assistance"; Herb wrote a lyric for a song about "Mary, Queen of Scots"; and Dorothy starred. It was such a hit with its audience that it was reprised at the Cort Theatre on a Sunday evening in April.

Theatre Magazine, which also ran a photo, wrote that the "tuneful, rollicking musical comedy" had lyrics by Lorenz Hart and a "delightful score by Richard C. Rodgers . . . . The cast included Miss Dorothy Fields, daughter of Lew Fields; Miss Ella Le Blang, Miss Elise Bonwit of the Metropolitan Ballet; Miss Ethel Rogers, daughter of Maude Raymond, and many other clever and talented young people. . . ."

Herb also collaborated with Rodgers and Hart on the Columbia Varsity Show, staging the dances. (Larry Hart had already left Columbia, but was still eligible for the show. When they submitted their entry to the jury, it was to recent Columbia grad Oscar Hammerstein II, who was just having his first Broadway success.) *Fly with Me*, the Varsity Show of 1920, was a raging hit, and led to a follow-up Varsity entry, and to Lew engaging Rodgers and Hart to supply the score for his next show, *Poor Little Ritz Girl*; that show's hit tune turned out to be, ironically, Herb's lone lyric, for "Mary, Queen of Scots."

Together, the three friends wrote *The Melody Man*, a sentimental play with songs, and combined their names so the author's credit read "Herbert Richard Lorenz." Lew went on to produce and star in it himself, in 1924 (it also featured a young Fredric March). Out of town, they ran out of money, and Larry Hart's father cajoled his friend Billy Rose into putting in the missing $1,000. Despite all the effort and Lew Fields's name, it flopped anyway.

After working on the *Garrick Gaieties*, initially a Theatre Guild benefit extended on its wild success (it contained "Manhattan," an enormous hit that put Rodgers and Hart on the national map), Herb wrote the libretto for the trio's first book musical, *Dearest Enemy*

(Lew passed as producer, having been burned the last time). Lew may have been sorry, because this time they had a solid triumph. In the years following 1925, Lew responded by producing their next five shows—the first three of which, *The Girl Friend* (1926), *Peggy-Ann* (1926), and *A Connecticut Yankee* (1927), were also big hits. (In addition, he produced Herb's 1927 effort with, among others, Vincent Youmans, *Hit the Deck*, an even bigger hit.)

Herb's quick wit, facility with words, and sense of theatre, whether as writer, director, choreographer, or any of the other roles he played apprenticing on amateur shows had all come together at a time when he could guide his father into a new lease on the elder's venerable career. Herb was a prototype of the kind of youthful, urban, jazz-age sophisticate the Rodgers and Hart shows typified— in sensibility, and in the kind of audience they attracted. For Lew, whose brand of musical comedy was of the Weber and Fields dialect-and-custard-pie variety, the musical theatre had become a strange new world. Like the Gershwins, Fields, Rodgers, and Hart had been tremendously influenced by the Princess Theatre shows, in which Jerome Kern, P. G. Wodehouse, and Guy Bolton had brought musical comedy out of nineteenth-century European operetta and into twentieth-century America, with modern settings and characters, topical plots, and scaled-down production values. Ever tuned in to the need to keep up with the times, Lew allowed Herb to be his eyes and ears. Herb continued to worship his father, and was living in the great man's shadow. (For his part, Lew never openly acknowledged Herb's homosexuality, though apparently he was aware of it.)

In the midst of this world—an attractive, gung-ho gang of "kids" forever "putting on a show"—Dorothy was growing up. She and Dick Rodgers even dated for a bit, strolling through the park holding hands. Dorothy was a ladylike, though snappy addition to that theatrical smart set. In turn, it was a tremendous influence on her.

Successful librettist Herbert Fields

Upon finishing school, her gravitation toward the family business (particularly her wish to go onstage) was rebuffed vigorously by both parents, and she worked for awhile as a teacher (of drama, at her alma mater) and a lab technician. Lew, in fact, squashed an opportunity she had for acting in summer stock at a playhouse in Tarrytown, New York, by intercepting a letter of acceptance. Then one day she was on the golf course with a cousin in Woodmill, Long Island, and met J. Fred Coots. From that moment, despite the best efforts of Lew and Rose, everything would change.

J. FRED COOTS was a songwriter and plugger at Jack Mills Music, Inc. music publishers. On the evening of their golf course introduction, he and Dorothy sat around the piano. He played some of his songs (among the standards he'd write would be "You Go to My Head" and "Santa Claus Is Coming to Town"); Dorothy (who was quite proficient at the keyboard) played the Rodgers tunes she'd known since Dick had been writing them, and Coots asked her if she'd ever thought of writing lyrics. In fact, she had been doing some light verse—"society" or "smarty" verse, as it was also called—and had been published in Franklin P. Adams's column, "The Conning Tower," in the New York *World* (as had other Sunday verse writers like Ira Gershwin).

Coots urged her to try some lyrics. They wrote a few songs together, but the things they came up with didn't excite either of them. Dorothy would later recall, "The music was good, but the lyrics were terrible." A lot of the problem, she realized, was that she was spending more energy trying to imitate Larry Hart than on focusing her own instincts. "I was so impressed with Larry's inner rhyming and feminine hybrid rhymes that I wasn't doing anything but trying to be like Larry, and consequently, mine weren't very good."

Even though it became apparent that their own partnership was going nowhere, Coots began introducing Dorothy to a round of music publishers on Tin Pan Alley. Now, Tin Pan Alley is more a mythical state of mind than an actual geographical location. However, in the early part of the century, the music publishing business did center on a string of publishing houses along Manhattan's West 28th Street, and in the 1920s followed the heart of the theatre district up Broadway to the 40s. There, cubicle after cubicle of cigar-smoking hacks (and also some excellent songwriters making their beginnings) pounded out tunes on tinny upright pianos, while lyricists wedded to them by the publisher sat by and helped churn out finished songs.

This was the picture in Lew Fields's mind as his younger daughter announced to the family her desire to enter the world of songwriting. It didn't take him a moment to decide that after the care he and Rose had taken to make their family life a bastion of respectability in a show business swamp, this was out of the question. His elder daughter had already married into a decent and good family, and he and Rose had the same plans for Dorothy, who'd been raised to be every bit as much a lady as Frances (although Dorothy had benefited from the loosened parental scrutiny that came from being born on the other side of two brothers). The thought of her in those smoke-filled offices demonstrating her wares to leering managers and vaudevillians stopping by to pick up some new material was too much for Lew. So he did the only thing he thought a good father should do. He used his influence with a number of prominent publishers to prevent her from being hired. Coots continued to introduce Dorothy around, and everywhere was met with the same "Well if she's so damn talented, why doesn't her father do anything for her?"

Eventually, however, Coots brought her to Jack Mills Music, Inc., where Mills decided to give her a chance. In those days, publishers commissioned popular songs to commemorate any occasion they thought would make the public buy sheet music, particularly if it involved a national hero, say, Lindbergh or Valentino; when Enrico Caruso died, overnight there was a song called "They Needed a Songbird in Heaven, So God Took Caruso Away." In 1924, on the heels of her introduction to Mills Music, Dorothy got a call from Jack Mills. It seemed that Ruth Elder, the aviatrix, was about to beat Lindbergh and make the first solo flight over the Atlantic. He needed a song overnight, he said, to commemorate the event. It was to be called "Our American Girl." Dorothy would be paid fifty dollars. She recalled later, "He said, 'I'll even give you the

Right page: Dorothy in the 1920s. The publicist's blurb reads "Dorothy Fields, lyricist of *Blackbirds* and the *International Revue*, has just left for Hollywood to do a picture."

first two lines: 'You took a notion to fly 'cross the ocean / Our American girl.'" I said, 'Mr. Mills, you don't just "take a notion to fly 'cross the ocean."'" Despite her objection that it made no sense, Mills was adamant. The next morning she turned in her lyric for "Our American Girl." It was never published, because Ruth Elder never made it. But Dorothy did receive her fifty dollars, as she would for similar overnight assignments, until she became known around the business as "the fifty-dollar-a-night girl."

The professional manager at Mills was a gregarious Boston Irishman named Jimmy McHugh. McHugh was a successful song-writer in his own right (with hit tunes like "When My Sugar Walks Down the Street") and had begun as a plugger, a staff pianist riding around Boston on a special bicycle with a key-board built onto it, playing the latest hope-to-be hits all over town. At night he would go to the nightclubs, saloons, and other gathering places and play them again, trying to hook and sell the public.

McHugh was a naturally gift-ed pianist and musician, able to improvise and transpose from one key to another effortlessly. From a lower-middle-class Irish-Catholic family, he'd been taught by his mother, who used to rap him on the knuckles when he didn't play something properly. He'd been offered a scholarship at the New England Conservatory of Music, but turned it down because of the constraints he felt in that formalized atmosphere. Besides, he was as much a salesman as a musician, with the gift of gab and a cocky, street-smart style.

He suggested to Dorothy that they try a song together, wanting to see how she'd do putting lyrics to an original tune, rather than simply feeding them to the publishing house to be matched with existing ones, which is how her assignments had been going.

Their first effort turned out to be a successful one. Called "Collegiana," it owed its existence to the "rah rah" college culture craze, the Charleston, and, very specifically, to De Sylva, Brown, and Henderson's "Varsity Drag." Dorothy still showed the influ-ence of her heroes Larry Hart and Ira Gershwin (slangy, smarty

Hit songwriting team of Dorothy Fields and Jimmy McHugh

interior rhymes), but this time her own voice began to show through:

> On the campus they try to vamp us
> With anything new, or anything blue;
> My diploma is now in a coma,
> My studying too is pretty near thru.
>
> I've found a new collegiate hop,
> Dance til I drop, I never stop;
> If you want to see what is getting me,
> I'll show you how to do:

And the chorus went on:

> Collegiana, see how it's done,
> Easy as pie and lots of fun,
> You never have to study
> This muddy water hop;
>
> Miss Pollyanna never was glad
> Until she grabbed an undergrad
> And did Collegiana,
> It never was a flop.
>
> Honor students and every pedagogue
> All go to bed agog at night,
> Two step, new step, you step along with me,
> You'll get a new degree dancing!
>
> You're gonna burn up, turn up your heel,
> Air your books, you'll begin to feel
> You know the new Hosanna,
> Collegiana reel.

As Dorothy liked to say later, "I think it was the 'pedagogue/bed agog' rhyme that got Jimmy." It was their first hit.

Soon afterward, McHugh, who had an in to write some songs for Harlem's Cotton Club, asked Dorothy to collaborate. If McHugh was twelve years older than his now twenty-two-year-old lyricist, that was only the beginning of their differences. He was outgoing and street smart, she was shy and timid, a lady who was not yet one of the boys. At the same time, they were able to hammer out a cordial working relationship that would last a decade and produce hundreds of songs, including some of the most long-lasting standards in the American songbook. And as unlikely a pair as they were, there was nothing that was going to stop Dorothy from taking him up on his offer to collaborate on the Cotton Club job.

When, gathered around the dinner table with her family, she announced that she would be writing songs for the Cotton Club, her parents were predictably aghast. "That really set the family off," she recalled. Lew responded with, "The *what* Club?" And as she tried to explain, he countered with the admonition that ladies didn't write lyrics, to which she responded, in a send-up of his own Weber and Fields gag, "I'm not a lady, I'm your daughter." In the story she loved to repeat throughout her life, she went on to say that she'd write lyrics for the Westminster Kennel Club if she was given the chance. For the moment, there was nothing more for Lew or Rose to say.

Located at Lenox Avenue and 142nd Street in the center of Harlem, the famed Cotton Club was the trendy uptown nightspot that featured the cream of black performers entertaining well-heeled downtown white patrons. They trekked uptown in droves, lured by the exotic promise of a chorus line made up exclusively of "copper colored beauties" and stars like Bill "Bojangles" Robinson and musicians like the not-yet-famous Duke Ellington, who would make his New York debut in the same "Hot Chocolates" revue for which Fields and McHugh had come up to write songs. In a manner that mirrored the disparities of the restrictive-yet-hedonistic 1920s, the Cotton Club and the all-black revues that began to move downtown to Broadway were a peculiar amalgam of racial segregation and a genuine opportunity for black performers to shine and be appreciated by white New York audiences.

The club (it being during prohibition) was owned by gangsters, specifically Owney Madden and Herman Stark. Stark kept pet pigeons, to which he was very attached, on the club's roof; when serving time in prison, he had become acquainted with the pigeons that had perched on the windowsill of his cell, at the time considering them his only friends.

As the only woman hanging around at rehearsals among the creative team, musicians, and club characters, Dorothy was treated with kid gloves. "I must say all the boys were simply wonderful," she recalled. "I was the little sister. They were very solicitous of me, very careful not to say anything wrong in front of me, and they got furious if anyone used improper language in my presence. No one was allowed to say 'Darn.' During afternoon rehearsals, they'd go into the kitchen and bring out cookies and tea."

For the revue, Dorothy and McHugh wrote the songs "Hottentot Tot," "Freeze an' Melt," and "Harlemania." Opening night, December 4, 1927, was packed with a glittering crowd, including the entire Fields family and Lew's friend, the columnist Walter Winchell. Sitting around the table with Dorothy and McHugh, they all watched in excitement as the team's first song came up. The singer, Aida Ward, began the song, but rather than sing the lyrics Dorothy had written, as Dorothy later recalled, "She belted out three of the most shocking, ribald, bawdy, dirtiest songs anyone had ever heard in the 1920s. I looked at McHugh, McHugh looked at me, my father didn't look at my mother; my brothers and sister looked down at their plates; and nobody dared look at Walter Winchell. My father said, 'You didn't learn those words home.' I said, 'I didn't write those words.'"

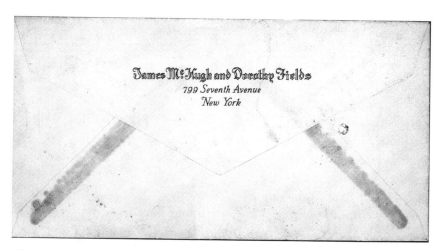

The team's official letterhead

The Cotton Club, in Harlem's heyday

Lew Fields, in a rage, went to find one of the owners, and supposedly threatened to take him outside if he didn't correct the situation. (Considering that Madden's full name was Owney "the Killer," the manner of Fields's threat is questionable, though he certainly made his anger felt.) The club promptly made an announcement that the song that Miss Ward had just sung had not been written by Fields and McHugh.

Building on their Cotton Club experience, McHugh talked impresario Harry Delmar, who produced a revue called *Delmar's Revels*, into letting them write some numbers for his next show. Delmar needed a song that would be a quick verse and chorus "in one"—that is, with the actors in front of the curtain while the scene was being changed—to introduce a "parade number," in which the curtains would part, and down the stairs would come showgirls, scantily clad, but bejeweled wherever there was room. For the song, Dorothy and McHugh dug out something they'd already written but never used, altered the title, spruced up the lyrics, and it was given to the unknown Bert Lahr and Patsy Kelly. The song was "I Can't Give You Anything but Love." Lahr (the great comedian most widely remembered as the *Wizard of Oz*'s Cowardly Lion) and Kelly played two poor kids, and he sang it to her as they sat on the

JIMMY MCHUGH WAS AN OUTGOING, GREGARIOUS MAN

who knew as much about selling a song as writing one. A natural musical talent, he had entered the workforce as an office boy with the Boston Opera where he heard Galli-Curci, Tetrazzini, and Caruso sing the operatic repertory (he remained a Puccini fan all his life) and, picking up the music by ear, would turn around and play it with a beat. From there he went on as a song plugger to Irving Berlin's publishing house and then to Mills Music where he eventually became a partner and met Dorothy. After he and Dorothy dissolved their partnership in the mid-1930s, he'd continue to have a successful career with other lyricists (particularly Harold Adamson) until his death in 1969.

"He always had something going on in his mind," says Lucille Meyers, who came to McHugh as a secretary in 1945 and on his death took over the administration of his estate. "He would write down music on a napkin in a restaurant. One story goes that when he wrote 'I Couldn't Sleep a Wink Last Night,'" it was because he couldn't sleep so he took a pencil and wrote it on his bedsheet. The next day at the studio he couldn't remember the song (it was for Frank Sinatra's first picture, *Higher and Higher*), so he called his housekeeper to tell her to messenger over the sheet, but it had already gone to the laundry. So they had to get it back from the laundry."

Fields and McHugh's first hit, 1928. Harry Delmar had previously thrown the song out of his *Revels*.

Blackbirds of 1928

with
UKULE[LE]
ARRANGE[MENT]

I CAN'T GIVE YOU ANYTHING [BUT LOVE]
I MUST HAVE THAT [MAN]
DIG A DIG A D[IG]
DOIN' THE NEW LOW [DOWN]
SHUFFLE YOUR FEET AND R[OLL]
BANDANNA BABIE[S]
HERE COMES MY BLAC[KBIRD]
DIXIE

Lyrics by
DOROTHY FIELDS
Music by
JIMMY McHUGH

I CAN'T GIVE YOU ANYTHING BUT LOVE

Gee, but it's tough to be broke,
  kid,
It's not a joke, kid, it's a curse;
My luck is changing, it's gotten
From simply rotten, to some-
  thing worse.

Who knows some day I will win
  too,
I'll begin to reach my prime;
Now though I see what our end
  is
All I can spend is just my time.

I can't give you anything but
  love, baby,

That's the only thing I've plenty
  of, baby,
Dream awhile, scheme awhile,
We're sure to find,
Happiness and I guess
All those things you've always
  pined for,

Gee, I'd like to see you looking
  swell, baby,
Diamond bracelets Woolworth
  doesn't sell, baby,
Till that lucky day, you know
  darned well, baby,
I can't give you anything but
  love.

ALONG WITH BEING A PERFORMER, MICHAEL FEINSTEIN

is a dedicated archival aficionado of the American popular song, seeking out associations with composers and lyricists wherever there is interesting information to be gleaned, as with Sammy Cahn, the irrepressible lyricist of countless hits like "Call Me Irresponsible," "Teach Me Tonight," and "The Tender Trap."

"Sammy Cahn used to quote the lyric for 'I Must Have That Man,'" he recalls. "I remember being at his house one night, and he said, 'You want to hear a perfect lyric?' He said, 'This is a perfect song.' And he sang 'I Must Have That Man,' and went line for line through that song. And he demonstrated as only a songwriter can demonstrate a song—as though he had written it. I just remember him relishing each line. He spoke of the economy of expression, the eloquence and yet simplicity. I remember him especially going, '"I'm like an oven that's cryin' for heat"—what a line!'"

I MUST HAVE THAT MAN

Don't want my mammy, I don't
   need a friend,
My heart is broken, it won't ever
   mend,
I ain't much carin' just where I
   will end,
I must have that man!

I'm like a oven that's cryin' for
   heat,
He treats me awful each time
   that we meet,
It's just unlawful how that boy
   can cheat,
But I must have that man!

He's hot as Hades,
A lady's not safe in his arms
   when she's kissed,
But I'm afraid that he's cooled off
And maybe I'm ruled off his list,
I'll never be missed

I need that person much
   worse n' just bad,
I'm half alive, n' he's drivin' me
   mad,
He's only human, if he's to be
   had
I must have that man!

stoop of a tenement. (Some speculate that the song was originally "I Can't Give You Anything but Love, Lindy," and that the two had written it for the aviator; on the other hand, Dorothy later said she got it from the conversation she and McHugh had overheard of a poor black couple standing wistfully in front of Tiffany's window, which the man ended by uttering something like "Gee, honey, I can't give you . . ." at which point Dorothy and McHugh rushed home and finished the song in an hour.)

In any case, on the opening night of *Delmar's Revels*, the song was a disaster. Harry Delmar hated it so much that after the one performance he told them, "Take your song and get it out of the theatre." They did.

They would try again with it in their next show. Spinning off their Cotton Club work, they were hired to write the songs for another revue, Lew Leslie's *Blackbirds of 1928*. *Blackbirds* was one of the all-black revues that were filtering downtown from Harlem and onto Broadway, becoming all the rage. Like the Cotton Club shows, they were mostly written and produced by whites for whites. Billed as "A Distinctive and Unique Entertainment," *Blackbirds* was a collection of songs and sketches that showcased, according to the program:

—

LYRICS BY DOROTHY FIELDS
MUSIC BY JIMMY MCHUGH

*with an all-star cast of one
hundred colored artists*

Featuring

Adelaide Hall   Bill Robinson

Aida Ward   Tim Moore

Blackbird Beauty Chorus
and the
Plantation Orchestra

Allie Ross, Conductor

Entire production staged and conceived by Mr. Lew Leslie

—

After a tryout in Atlantic City, *Blackbirds* opened in New York at the Liberty Theatre on May 9, 1928, to abysmal reviews. One of them went out of its way to mention "a sickly, puerile song called, 'I Can't Give You Anything but Love.'" Lew Fields asked his daughter, "Well, are you satisfied? Now will you get out of show business?"

Nevertheless, producer Lew Leslie kept the show running, even with the anemic business it was doing. The sketches were written by Leslie, and looking back from the post–civil rights world, the show doesn't seem likely to be revived anytime soon, with entries like "Aunt Jemima Stroll" and "Scene in Jungle Land." But the first full score that Fields and McHugh had ever written was remarkably strong and sustained. Besides the "sickly, puerile song," Dorothy and McHugh had written a number of others that would go on to wide popular success. (A few years before the Gershwins would get to it, there was also a "Porgy" number, based on the DuBose Heyward play.) "Doin' the New Low Down" was written at the last minute and introduced by Bill Robinson and the Blackbird Chorus, and was another "dance-craze-and-this-is-how-you-do-it" kind of song so prevalent in the 1920s.

> I got my feet to misbehavin' now
> I got a soul that's not for savin' now
> Heigh! Ho! Doin' the New Low Down.

"Diga, Diga, Doo"—a "jungle" number with the idea that ". . . when you love it is natural to / Diga Diga Doo, Diga Doo Doo"—was a big popular hit. And the torchy, bluesy "I Must Have That Man" went on to become a standard, with its colloquial, black English in same vein as Kern and Hammerstein's "Can't Help Lovin' Dat Man of Mine."

> Don't want my mammy, I don't need a friend,
> My heart is broken, it won't ever mend,
> I ain't much carin' just where I will end,
> I must have that man!

In the *Blackbirds* songs, along with a wit that was at once urbane and earthy, Dorothy's growing deftness with language and in rhyming—especially the interior rhyming that would become an elegant trademark—was beginning to show itself.

One main reason that the songs were allowed to catch on the way they did was that eventually Leslie added (in addition to the regular Wednesday and Saturday matinees) a midnight show on Thursdays. Suddenly *Blackbirds* became *the* place in town to go and to be seen, and it ended an extremely successful run only after it had been going for 519 performances. It also had the distinction of being the first Broadway show to record an entire album—on which Bill Robinson and Adelaide Hall were joined by Ethel Waters and Duke Ellington's Orchestra.

The major success to come out of the show, however, was the previously disgraced "I Can't Give You Anything but Love." With fluid lines like "Gee I'd like to see you looking swell, baby" (subtle in its internal rhyming, juxtaposed with vernacular like "Gee," "swell," and "baby"), its catchy repetition of "baby," simple, yet slangy language, and its poignantly straightforward expression of flat-out broke-ness, the song struck a chord with the public (ahead of its time—a year later the stock market would crash). "I Can't Give You Anything but Love" went on to become such an enormous popular hit that in late 1928 there wasn't a piano in America that didn't have the sheet music sitting on top of it, or a phonograph that wasn't blaring the Number One chart record made by Cliff "Ukelele Ike" Edwards. The title became such a catchphrase that it appeared everywhere—from ads and cartoons to the cover of *Life*. It remains one of the most durable and oft-revived song hits of all time. After Edwards's original record, there was a cover record (a competing version) by Gene Austin; the tune was revived on the charts by Billie Holiday with Teddy Wilson in 1936, and again in 1948 by Rose Murphy. It was caught on celluloid in the movies *I Can't Give You Anything but Love Baby*, *True to the Army*, *Stormy Weather*, and *Jam Session*, and was given perhaps its most memorable performances in two nonmusical films—sung by Katharine Hepburn and

Cary Grant to a leopard on a roof in *Bringing Up Baby*, and hummed by Judy Holliday opposite an aggravated Broderick Crawford in the famous gin rummy scene from *Born Yesterday*. Since the original *Blackbirds*, the song has returned to Broadway in *Ain't Misbehavin'* and *Sugar Babies*.

For the songwriting team of Fields and McHugh, the end of 1928 meant they had arrived, and were in demand. And that Hollywood had begun to call. But for the moment they kept their attention on Broadway. They finished out the year collaborating on a Fields family venture called (appropriately) *Hello Daddy!* It starred and was produced by Lew Fields, with a score by Dorothy and McHugh and a book by Herbert, and opened at the Fields Theatre the day after Christmas. Lew had just come off his producing success on Rodgers and Hart's (and Herb's) *A Connecticut Yankee* and the less successful *Present Arms*, and *Hit the Deck!* *Hello Daddy!* was a thin farce adapted from a German play, about three men each supporting what he thinks is his own illegitimate child. (That premise would be remodeled and resurface decades later as the Gina Lollobrigida movie *Buona Sera, Mrs Campbell*, musicalized again on Broadway in the 1970s as Alan Jay Lerner and Burton Lane's ill-fated *Carmelina*.)

Hello Daddy! marked the last time that Lew Fields appeared onstage (after some four decades as a performer, he retired from the spotlight), and the first time that Dorothy worked on a book musical rather than simply contributed songs to a revue. But though it ran 197 performances (around six months) and launched Dorothy's fascination with developing the book musical, *Hello Daddy!* was hardly an achievement for the ages. She and McHugh supplied the songs "As Long as We're in Love," "Futuristic Rhythm," and "Let's Sit and Talk About You"; they wouldn't be remotely as popular as those from their last show, or the show that was to come afterward.

There were other shows to keep the team busy, like the two editions of the *Ziegfeld Midnight Frolic* they did that year, on the New Amsterdam roof. At the same time, in her personal life, Dorothy was in the process of ending her first marriage. In 1924

HELLO DADDY!

MUSICAL NUMBERS

Musical numbers played by Ben Pollack
and his Central Park Hotel Orchestra

Max Steiner, Conductor

The Entr'acte Music is conducted by Mr. Ben Pollack

SCENE 1

1. "Three Little Maids from School" ....Betty, Dot,
Grace and Ensemble

2. "I Want Plenty of You" ....Connie and Larry

3. "Futuristic Rhythm" ....Helen and Ensemble

SCENE 2

4. (a) "Let's Sit and Talk About You" ....Larry and Connie

   (b) Refrain ....Giersdorf Sisters

5. Reprise ....Larry and Connie

SCENE 3

6. "Party Line" ....Ensemble

7. "Your Disposition Is Mine" ....Connie, Larry and Ensemble

8. "In a Great Big Way" ....Betty, Noel and Ensemble

9. Finale ....Ensemble

ACT II

10. "Maybe Means Yes" ....Helen and Chorus

11. "As Long as We're in Love" . .Connie, Larry and Giersdorf Sisters

12. "Out Where the Blues Begin" ....Noel and Chorus

    Finale ....The Company

An early portrait

she had met and married Dr. Jack Wiener, a chest specialist on the staff of Montefiore Hospital, with a "Park Avenue" practice (though his office was located on 58th Street and he lived on Central Park South). Wiener, who was more than ten years her senior, had grown up in the Rockaway section of Queens, then a summer resort that emptied out in the wintertime. The son of a baker with ambitions for his children, Jack was one of three brothers and two sisters; while the sisters were married off and Jack was pursuing his medical education, one brother became a dentist, and the other a lawyer and eventually a judge. Handsome and tall, with black hair and blue eyes, Jack played tennis and ran with the social and show-business "in" crowd, palling around with Stork Club proprietor Sherman Billingsley, among other theatrical types.

Lew and Rose Fields were delighted when Dorothy and Jack told them of their intentions. The idea of their nineteen-year-old daughter marrying a successful Jewish doctor was just the kind of respectability they'd always worked for on behalf of themselves and their children. The elder Fieldses announced the engagement, with plans for a big wedding, as they'd given her sister, Frances. But rather than wait for her parents to return from Lew's tour with Joe Weber, as they'd agreed, Dorothy and Jack were married quietly in the home of an Upper West Side rabbi. It was Dorothy's way of being sensitive to her father's vulnerable financial situation and sparing him the expense of the lavish affair he would have insisted on giving her.

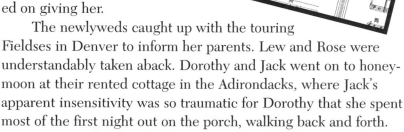

The newlyweds caught up with the touring Fieldses in Denver to inform her parents. Lew and Rose were understandably taken aback. Dorothy and Jack went on to honeymoon at their rented cottage in the Adirondacks, where Jack's apparent insensitivity was so traumatic for Dorothy that she spent most of the first night out on the porch, walking back and forth.

Jack, it seemed, was not the perfect match for her. He may have appeared to be a sophisticated, worldly mate for Dorothy, but reality played out differently. In fact, though his patients were said to love him, few other people followed suit. He and Dorothy didn't get along, it turned out, from the beginning. They stayed legally married for almost a decade, but practically from the honeymoon on, they lived completely separate lives, coming together for the occasional holiday and family function. (Jack's family, however, loved her. She was "Aunt Dotz" to his six-year-old nephew, Frank, and to the rest of the Wiener clan, whom she visited with her husband on occasions like Passover, and continued to keep track of after their eventual divorce.) Dorothy moved back into the Fields domicile, which was now a suite of apartments at 562 West End Avenue.

There, it was roiling with activity almost twenty-four hours a day. Herb was living there and working on the Rodgers and Hart shows; Lew and Rose presided over the family while Lew pursued the new lease on his producing career afforded by his mentoring of the Rodgers, Hart, and Fields team; Joe would return from Europe and the perfume business and finally break down and join the family business, to his parents' initial disappointment. Day and night, there was a constant stream of people in and out of the residence. And now, with his successful children contributing their not insignificant earnings, the Fields lifestyle was as extravagant as ever.

This was the atmosphere in which Dorothy had begun her work with Jimmy McHugh and transformed herself from an ex-aspiring actress and schoolteacher into one of the hottest young songwriters in the country, whose weekly earnings, within the next couple of years, would run into four figures.

As 1929 ended and the new decade began, MGM called. Since Al Jolson and *The Jazz Singer* had overwhelmingly ushered in the age of the talkies just two years earlier, the studios were clamoring to bring west the best Broadway talent to supply them with scores and hit songs for the newest rage—movie musicals. So with the lure of a disproportionately fat weekly paycheck, and the beckoning of glamorous life by the swimming pool (and still with Broadway projects pending), Dorothy and McHugh boarded a train for their first trip to the West Coast.

F IN THE 1920S the Gershwins, Rodgers and Hart, and their contemporaries were the first to export New York City sophistication to middle America with songs that were soaking into everyday consciousness, then the exodus to Hollywood of the brightest Broadway composers and lyricists beginning in the early 1930s escalated the process to a mass scale. Jerome Kern, the granddaddy of American popular song, went; so did Irving Berlin, Harold Arlen, E. Y. "Yip" Harburg, Oscar Hammerstein II—as well as the aforementioned George and Ira Gershwin, Rodgers and Hart (who soon turned around and headed back), and a slew of other talents that included Dorothy and Jimmy McHugh.

It was hard to blame them. First there was the money. Or more accurately, first there was the Depression. With the devastation of the American economy in 1929, the theatre, only a short hop uptown from Wall Street, was hit hard. As Joan Blondell, who opened on Broadway in *Maggie, the Magnificent* with James Cagney on the night the stock market crashed, would later say, "Nothing ran at that time because everybody was busy jumping out of windows." Audiences and backers alike who had lost their savings and jobs and were trying to adjust to the shock of those early days had other things on their minds. The day of giddy flapperdom and the six-day bicycle races that provided the backdrop for *The Girl Friend* were now officially obsolete. So was lavish production spectacle. The Broadway that would flourish over the next decade was very different as the changing times stimulated enormous evolution, like the social realism of the Group Theatre, and politically conscious playwrights like Clifford Odets and Lillian Hellman. The Depression did not prevent the rise of new musical talents like Cole Porter (Herb Fields's next major collaborator after Rodgers and Hart), but comedies and musicals as well took on a populist tone, and even when audiences sought escape, they went to the Gershwins' *Of Thee I Sing* and

Kaufman and Hart's *You Can't Take It with You*. Also, everyday people looking to forget their troubles for a couple of hours began overwhelmingly to head for the local movie palace, where stars were plentiful, the bill changed constantly, and you could lose yourself in a double feature, a cartoon, and a newsreel for a dime. Theatre had become, it seemed, a pricey diversion for the swells. In the 1929–30 season, of legit

John Barrymore.

theatres on Broadway between 42nd and 53rd streets, seventeen converted to showing movies (the Palace maintained vaudeville). Five thousand Broadway actors were out of work.

The Depression affected the Fields family directly on several levels. Lew now reconciled himself to the fact that he was finally completely out of touch with contemporary audiences, and after producing the *The Vanderbilt Revue* in 1930, which flopped after two weeks, he gave up producing (having retired from performing after *Hello Daddy!*) and ended his more than fifty-year professional career. Financially, as he had faced bankruptcy and money terrors on a recurring basis throughout his adult life, the crash did not bring anything new. (For one thing, Lew was never really solvent enough to have stock investments.)

Herbert, however, who had through his Rodgers and Hart collaborations become one of the most successful librettists on Broadway, was hurt significantly by the crash. One reason was that he'd invested heavily with his brother-in-law's firm. Frances's husband, Charles Marcus, had run the Bank of the United States, which had been founded by his father, and had, at the time of the crash, fifty-nine branches. During the '20s, he'd been edged out by his brother, Bernard, who had taken over the bank and wheeled and dealed it to enormous growth, keeping depositors' profits, manipulating stock transfers, and initiating other slippery mishandling of the bank's assets, most of which disappeared. When the bank collapsed in the heat of pursuit by the government, it was the largest bank collapse on record. Bernard and his partners would go to jail, and the square Charles, though no longer directly involved in the business, would be circumstantially sucked into the scandal and suffer indictment and a criminal trial.

Apart from the other traumas, Charles and Frances met financial ruin, and their lives were changed irrevocably. They were forced to give up their sumptuous Upper West Side apartment, servants, and amenities and exiled to mundane, suburban anonymity. Frances, with her rarefied upbringing, tried to adjust and take care of her children; her husband never recovered (they would eventually divorce).

The Marcuses' misfortunes were ironic in that, while Charles had been one to bail Lew out of his myriad financial scrapes, the rest of his family had always scorned the "disreputable, no-good, showbiz" Fields family. It was also ironic that shortly before the crash Charles had in good faith convinced the Fieldses to do something sensible and put away their money "safely" with the Bank of the United States—which is what led to Herb's heavy losses.

In Hollywood, though, business was booming. The sun shone all day every day, the parties were wild every night, and under the palm trees of Beverly Hills and Burbank, studio executives hustled to churn out enough product to fill the demand from movie houses across the country. It wasn't only composers and lyricists who were lured west by a combination of money, opportunity, the weather, and gracious living. In fact, the studios raided the best of New York's musical, theatrical, and literary communities to build up their organizations. Performers who'd been working onstage—like James Cagney, Jimmy Stewart, Bob Hope, Fred Astaire, Henry Fonda, Fredric March, Margaret Sullavan, and Katharine Hepburn—made the trip, as did writers F. Scott Fitzgerald, Dorothy Parker, and Lillian Hellman, among countless others. European giants of the Classical music world like Jascha Heifetz and Fritz Kreisler made a home there (along with Europeans in other disciplines, particularly directors), adding to the cosmopolitan social scene where intelligentsia mingled with newly minted movie stars.

Some of the songwriters who came out to reap their Hollywood offers hated it. Oscar Hammerstein—whose career had dipped some time after *Show Boat* and wouldn't fully recover until he teamed with Richard Rodgers for *Oklahoma!* in the early '40s—detested Hollywood, and though he lived and worked there a bit in the '30s, had relatively little success there. Rodgers and Hart also had limited accomplishment in Hollywood, though Larry Hart was quick to slip right into the party circuit. Others, like Burton Lane, who came out on a $250-a-week studio contract—a very comfortable paycheck in the depths of the Depression for anyone, let alone a songwriter—stayed there for decades. Later, Lane would return to New York to write shows like *Finian's Rainbow* in the 1940s. But most of his hit song writing and other work were done for the studios, where, teamed with lyricists like Ralph Freed and Harold Adamson, he turned out standards like "(I Like New York in June) How About You?" for movies like *Babes on Broadway* with Mickey Rooney and Judy Garland. Frank Loesser, too, before he made his theatre fame with *Guys and Dolls*, did a long tenure with the studios, producing songs like "Baby It's Cold Outside" (sung by Esther Williams and Ricardo Montalban in *Neptune's Daughter*).

The flip side of the perks that came with being on the studio payroll was less freedom than in the theatre. In the studio system, they told you what they needed, and you provided it—with no control over what happened to it. Some assignments would wind up as significant, cohesive scores destined to become classics, like Harold Arlen and Yip Harburg's for *The Wizard of Oz*; other work would go into forgettable musicals, or very often, the assignment was to supply a few songs to stick into an essentially nonmusical picture. (The other catch was that with the exception of a few lions like Jerome Kern, the studio owned the copyright on everything a songwriter did for them while on salary, diminishing future royalties for the composer or lyricist.)

When Dorothy and McHugh arrived on the coast, they both took to California living (McHugh never would return back east permanently). McHugh had facilitated their invitation to Hollywood because of his publishing connections, particularly with Jack

Robbins, who had envisioned the talent bazaar that studio-produced musicals would become, and set up shop as an adjunct to MGM, bringing them out. They'd taken the train out together for the three-day trip, working along the way and sidestepping the interruptions of McHugh's young son. They disembarked not in Los Angeles, but in Pasadena—which was the thing to do in those days, when stars (and others) returning home would avoid the crowds and be met by a car to drive them back to Beverly Hills or wherever it was they were going.

Dorothy and McHugh's agreement with the studio specified that they make themselves available for periods of several months at a time (which also allowed them to get back to New York to deal with the Broadway revues they were working on in 1930 and 1931). Their first documented film assignment, in 1930, was to provide the songs for *Love in the Rough*, a picture with a golf theme that starred Robert Montgomery and Dorothy Jordan. While the movie could hardly be referred to as a classic, the team came up with the songs "One More Waltz," "I'm Doin' That Thing," "Like Kelly Can," "I'm Learning a Lot from You," and "Go Home and Tell Your Mother"— which became a notable hit of 1930 with the chorus:

> Go home and tell your mother
> That she certainly did a wonderful job on you.
> Go home and tell your father
> That we're marryin' like respectable people do.
>
> Then ask her what she did
> Ask father what he did
> When both of them needed
> A darned sight more than kisses.
>
> Go home and tell your mother
> That her beautiful child is gonna belong to me.

They worked in an easy back-and-forth style. With McHugh's great facility, he'd spin out a melody either at the piano or humming

it on the move—along the street or traveling from one place to another—and
she would set it to words, often working by his side. When Dorothy was
asked which came first, the melody or
the lyrics, she liked to reply, "The
title." Titles, as well as ideas for
songs, came from either of them.
They both worked quickly, and
commonly finished a song in an
afternoon, or after working late into
the night.

They were so prolific that in 1934 Dorothy was touted
by journalist Mary Margaret McBride in a *New York World
Telegram* feature as celebrating the completion of her 500th song
lyric. (The score seems questionable.) In the article Dorothy calcu-
lated that to that point she'd used the word "love" some 5,000 times
in her lyrics, not including titles. Speaking also for every songwriter
colleague she ever had, she said, "I'm always looking for a new way
to say 'I love you.'" She went on, "You see, we phrase his love-mak-
ing for the boy who isn't very facile with words. We give him something that he can sing softly as he dances with his girl or sits in the
moonlight, soul racked with emotions he can't express. Suggestive
songs, by the way, never make great hits and the simply worded
ones go best."

Elaborating on the importance of a good title, she added, "It
has to be catchy and if possible contain some exciting new combination of familiar words used in a declarative sentence." In fact, Fields
titles generally do tend toward plain or slangy declarative state-
ments (or fragments), rather than the poetically abstracted: "I'm in
the Mood for Love," "You Couldn't Be Cuter," "If My Friends
Could See Me Now," "Nobody Does It Like Me." The
Hammerstein-Kern ballad was "All the Things You Are"; the Fields-
Kern ballad was specifically concerned with "The Way You Look
Tonight."

The poetry in—and hallmark of—a Fields ballad (though she
never considered her lyrics poetry) is in the perceptive eye for
detail, spoken matter-of-factly, that touches the precise truth of a
common human experience:

Someday, when I'm awfully low,
When the world is cold,
I will feel a glow just thinking of you
And the way you look tonight.

Her language and imagery are simple and
unsentimental, not high-flown, though the
expression, rhyming, and repetition are elegant. And her perspective is distinctly feminine.

    A few lyrics she did early on, in an
uncharacteristically fervent "poetic"
style, have worn less well relative to the
rest of her work. Forty years later,
Dorothy herself derided her lyric for
"Cuban Love Song," dissecting it
before an audience at the 92nd Street Y's Lyrics
and Lyricists series for symptoms of inexperience:

    "'I love you,
    That's what my heart is saying'

"Ridiculous! Your lips say the words. Your heart may dictate them,
but hearts don't talk, they beat. Second:

    'One melody will always thrill my heart,
    One kiss will cheer me when we're far apart'

"'One kiss will cheer me when we're far apart?' Neat trick, if you
can do it.

    'I love you
    With such a tender passion
    And only you could fashion
    Our Cuban love song.'

"'Fashion' and 'passion' rhyme, courtesy of Lorenz Hart."
    Nevertheless, "The Cuban Love Song" was one of the top hits
of 1931, and fed into the rhumba fever that was beginning to grip
the country (as did Kern and Otto Harbach's "The Night Was Made

THE YEAR "CUBAN LOVE SONG" APPEARED, 1931,

was the same that "The Star Spangled Banner" officially became the U.S. national anthem. Latin America was on everybody's hips as rhumba rhythms began inching their way north through the 1930s. "Cuban Love Song" was soon joined by many others like "The Carioca" and "Cuban Pete," introduced by the young sensation Desi Arnaz.

Fields and McHugh's effort, written for Lawrence Tibbett, who starred as a U.S. marine in the film *The Cuban Love Song,* was tailored to the Metropolitan Opera singer's heroic baritone. The ardent expression of the song is miles from their jazzy, jaunty hallmarks "I Can't Give You Anything but Love" and "On the Sunny Side of the Street." Dorothy's usual colloquial touch is supplanted by more exalted phrasings, like "That's what my heart is saying / While every breeze is playing . . ." etc.—which caused her later in life to single out the lyric as one that showed her inexperience.

If it comes across a bit high flown today, when it came out, "Cuban Love Song" was an enormous hit. Apart from Tibbett's movie rendition, the song was recorded by Paul Whiteman and his orchestra, as well as by Ruth Etting.

Met opera star Lawrence Tibbett, Jimmy Durante, and Ernest Torrence in *The Cuban Love Song,* 1931

CUBAN LOVE SONG

Life is filled with glory
Now that I know this love was
    meant to be.
Each kiss tells the story
While my heart rings and sings
    our melody
Dear,

I love you
That's what my heart is saying
While ev'ry breeze is playing
Our Cuban love song

I love you,
For all the joy you brought me
The lovely night you taught me
Our Cuban love song.

One melody will always thrill my
    heart
One kiss will cheer me when
    we're far apart,

Dear one,

I love you
With such a tender passion
And only you could fashion
Our Cuban love song.

for Love" and Herman Hupfeld's "When Yuba Plays the Rhumba on the Tuba"). From a picture by the same name, "Cuban Love Song" was written for Metropolitan Opera star baritone Lawrence Tibbett, who with his dashing matinee idol looks had launched a Hollywood career the previous year playing a bandit in *The Rogue Song*, MGM's Technicolor version of Franz Lehar's operetta *Gypsy Love*. *The Cuban Love Song* was the first of Dorothy's "opera singer" assignments, in which she provided material for Met stars gone Hollywood, like Lily Pons and Grace Moore. Released in 1931, *The Cuban Love Song* was a melodrama in the *Madame Butterfly* vein about a marine who while on leave in Cuba falls in love with a beautiful native girl, and later returns to retrieve his illegitimate child.

Besides the title song, Dorothy and McHugh contributed another called "Tramps at Sea." But the really memorable aspect of *The Cuban Love Song* was the international furor it created, which came to a head when MGM applied for a permit from the Hays office executive Joseph Breen to reissue the picture in 1937. First, with the Production Code having come into its own since the looser days of 1931, the censors didn't want to reissue the film at all, writing to MGM: "The story of illicit sex and illegitimacy seems to be treated without the proper compensating moral values required by the Code."

More important, *The Cuban Love Song* was creating outrage and unrest throughout Latin America. The foreign manager for the Motion Picture Producers and Distributors of America, Frederick L. Herron, wrote to the Breen office from New York:

> "I am having a Hell of a time with *The Cuban Love Song*. It has caused more trouble than you can possibly imagine, not only from the Cubans, but from the whole of the Latin American Consular Corps here . . . .
>
> To start with, Cuba hates Mexico, and always has. Lupe Velez's accent is Mexican, as are the accents of many people in the picture; it is distinctly different

from the Cuban accent. No Cubans I have ever talked to have ever seen a cart in the streets of Havana such as Lupe Velez uses in the picture. The words *"gringo"* and *"cochina"* are Central American, and the Cubans all say that they have never heard them used in Cuba. . . . It will take a long time to live down the conflagration that this picture has caused. . . ."

When the movie was being made, however, Dorothy and McHugh's minds were more domestically oriented—both to the chore of simply supplying songs the studio wanted, and to minding the Broadway projects they still had going back east.

There were four such projects, three of them revues, that were produced in 1930 and '31, and the team shuttled back to New York to give them attention. With *Blackbirds of 1928* still running, Lew Leslie set out to try and top his previous success, and he mounted *Lew Leslie's International Revue* (he'd also try a *Blackbirds of 1930*, with lyrics by Andy Razaf and music by Eubie Blake and featuring Ethel Waters, but it would fail after two months). The idea was that the *International Revue* would be kind of a musical League of Nations with songs and sketches delivered by stars Gertrude Lawrence, over from London, Broadway's Harry Richman, comedian Jack Pearl doing his Baron Munchausen radio character, and a Spanish dancer (from Spain) named Argentinita. Busby Berkeley was one of the choreographers.

The show stimulated great expectations, and had a sumptuous production that cost over 200,000 Depression dollars. But unfortunately, much of the material, though smartly topical, was thin. And long. On opening night the final curtain didn't come down till 12:15 A.M. The real disaster turned out to be Argentinita, who'd been hired sight unseen to make her American debut. On arrival, she turned out to be a matronly, hefty woman of questionable talent. Her forty or so minutes in the show engendered such hostility from the crowds that Leslie paid her a cool $10,000 to vacate the premises. Even without her, the show only ran ninety-five performances—about three months.

TYPICAL OF THE BEST FIELDS AND MCHUGH SONGS OF THE 1920S,

"Exactly Like You" was introduced on Broadway by Harry Richman and Gertrude Lawrence in *Lew Leslie's International Revue* of 1930. Dorothy later remembered the experience primarily for the trouble with Argentinita, the zaftig Spanish dancer Leslie had imported, who was such a flop with audiences that she had to be paid off just to leave. The show also yielded one of their biggest lifetime hits, "On the Sunny Side of the Street." "Exactly Like You" was popularized by Richman, as well as Ruth Etting, who also recorded it, before Benny Goodman and his orchestra picked it up a few years later and gave it new life.

EXACTLY LIKE YOU

I used to have a perfect sweet-
  heart,
Not a real one, just a dream,
A wonderful vision
Of us as a team.
Can you imagine how I feel now,
Love is real now, it's ideal
You're just what I wanted
And now it's nice to live,
Paradise to live

I know why I've waited
Know why I've been blue,
Prayed each night for someone
Exactly like you.

Why should we spend money
On a show or two
No one does those love scenes
Exactly like you,

You make me feel so grand
I want to hand the world to you
You seem to understand
Each foolish little scheme I'm
  scheming,
Dream I'm dreaming,

Now I know why mother
Taught me to be true
She meant me for someone
Exactly like you.

Sheet music for "Exactly Like You," 1930

The two notable respites in the *International Revue* came in the Fields and McHugh score. They'd written "International Rhythm" and the crash-referencing "The Margineers" ("We'll be in the American Can in the morning. . . ."). They also wrote "On the Sunny Side of the Street" and "Exactly Like You," which immediately went on to become two of the top hits of 1930. While "Exactly Like You" secured a place as a standard, "On the Sunny Side of the Street" would become not only an optimistic counterpart to "Brother, Can You Spare a Dime" in the Depression anthem sweepstakes, but—regardless of elapsed decades—one of the most universally recognizable popular songs ever written. (Apart from all its other exposure, it would go on to be featured in no less than seven movies.)

For *The Vanderbilt Revue*, producer Lew Fields called on his now stellar baby daughter to contribute songs (with McHugh) to what he hoped would be a comeback hit for him. The show had a talented young cast that included Lulu McConnell, Joe Penner (who'd become famous on radio for his line "Wanna buy a duck?"), and a young actress, Francesca Braggiotti, who later became more famous as the socialite wife of Ambassador Henry Cabot Lodge. Among the contributors to the score besides Dorothy and McHugh were Yip Harburg, Ned Washington (later responsible for "I'm Getting Sentimental Over You" and "When You Wish Upon a Star"), and Cole Porter.

Again, however, the notices were disappointing, and the people stayed away. Thirteen performances after it opened at the Vanderbilt Theatre on November 5, 1930, it closed. Even so, out of the four songs they contributed, Dorothy and McHugh had one of the year's notable hits with "Blue Again." *Vanderbilt*'s closing precipitated Lew Fields's total retirement from show business (that is, until Hollywood requested his services). When his son Herb and Rodgers and Hart offered him *America's Sweetheart*, their next project (based on their foray into Hollywood), he passed on it.

Shoot the Works, to which Dorothy and McHugh were asked to contribute, opened in July of 1931. It was the brainchild of columnist Heywood Broun, who arranged a cooperative venture with the purpose of giving work to unemployed actors, singers, dancers, and technicians. It cost $6,000 (of contributions) to open, and only performers and crew were to be paid. Broun appeared as master of ceremonies, and the creative team who contributed the revue's material included a number of the Algonquin Round Table/*New Yorker* set, such as Dorothy Parker, Nunnally Johnson, Peter Arno, and E. B. White, who were credited with the sketches; songs came from Irving Berlin, Ira Gershwin, Leo Robin, Jay Gorney, Yip Harburg, Vernon Duke, and Fields and McHugh (who contributed "How's Your Uncle?"). Directed by Theodore Hammerstein, Oscar Hammerstein's cousin, the cast included fledgling stars Imogene Coca and George Murphy, and although the show didn't win raves, it did provide eleven weeks of work for the performers and crew.

Fields and McHugh's last foray into Broadway as a team would come with their contribution of two songs to a play with music, *Singin' the Blues*, a "negro" play by John McGowan. The songs— "It's the Darndest Thing" and "Singin' the Blues" (with an additional one by Burton Lane and Harold Adamson)—were featured in

The Depression revue *Shoot the Works*, modeled after the wildly successful Garment Workers Union show *Pins and Needles*

"What I Like Best About Dorothy Fields

is her use of colloquialism and her effortlessness, as in 'Sunny Side of the Street,' which is just perfect as a lyric."

—Stephen Sondheim

ON THE SUNNY SIDE OF THE STREET

Walked with no-one, and talked
  with no-one,
And I had nothing but shadows
Then one morning you passed
And I brightened at last
Now I greet the day, and com-
  plete the day
With the sun in my heart
All my worry blew away
When you taught me how to say:

Grab your coat, and get your hat
Leave your worry on the
  doorstep
Just direct your feet
To the sunny side of the street.

Can't you hear a pitter pat?
And that happy tune is your step
Life can be so sweet
On the sunny side of the street,

I used to walk in the shade
With those blues on parade
But I'm not afraid
This rover crossed over,

If I never have a cent
I'll be rich as Rockefeller
Gold dust at my feet
On the sunny side of the street.

Spanish bomb "Argentinita" in *Lew Leslie's International Revue,* 1930

Jimmy McHugh in his newfound home, away from his native Boston weather and Tin Pan Alley. He would never leave California.

nightclub scenes. (It seemed to be ethnic-play week on Broadway; just six days before *Singin' the Blues* opened, so did *The Singing Rabbi*. *Blues* ran forty-six performances; *Rabbi* expired at four.)

The disjointed nature of her revue work—the idea of just contributing a few "random" songs that could be stuck in, taken out, or conceivably moved around—was not lost on Dorothy. So far, almost all her work had been in this vein. The baptism by fire that her Broadway experience had provided, being thrown into the do-or-die fray where she was required to produce on demand, had made her a consummate professional—she knew and appreciated that. Still, she yearned to tackle the more fulfilling accomplishment of a book show, where songs would be integral to the action, develop the characters, and further a total dramatic experience. "Writing for a revue, you start from scratch twelve or fourteen times," she would say later, referring to each number in one show. "After writing all those extraneous songs—pop songs, which was hard—I always thought writing a book show would be heaven."

It would be years, though, before she would turn her attention to those aspirations. For the time being, her life was becoming increasingly embedded in Hollywood. Beginning in 1932, Dorothy, still under fat contract with MGM, and Herbert, in a similarly cushy arrangement with Warner Brothers, rented the first of four houses in Beverly Hills that would be the Fields family base through the '30s.

If the rest of the country was being crushed by the Great Depression, Beverly Hills was the place to be. At the time it was the fastest-growing town in the country, with a population of about 25,000, and a new house completed every day. The movie industry people who inhabited the mansions that lined the palm-shaded streets could wait out the Depression in deck chairs by the tiled swimming pools, exerting themselves only to get up for a trip to the wet bar or an impromptu game of tennis. Of course, the writers, composers, directors, stars, and producers did work (and with shooting schedules, hard, too), but the pace, the style, and above all, the financial rewards couldn't be further from the way things were in New York—especially at the moment. You may have had to write to studio specifications, or not have had the control over what happened to your work that you had on Broadway, but on the other hand, you had much less of the responsibility, and oh, that paycheck. It was, to paraphrase *Porgy and Bess*, always summertime, and the livin' was easy.

Dorothy and Herb Fields personified the kind of "golden people" who drove this world—young, vibrant, talented, witty, smart, successful, extravagant. Soon after their arrival, older brother Joe, who'd gone to work for Republic on a $300-a-week contract to write B pictures, moved in with them. Up until recently, the money from his perfume business had made him the financially successful one in the family; the stock crash had changed all that.

Their lavish home, with servants and never fewer than four cars in the driveway, became the kind of social and creative Grand Central station that the family's New York apartment had been, with friends and colleagues of every description (but mostly the gifted and beautiful) coming and going at all hours: card games in one room, work or play around the piano in another, drinks on the porch, and pool parties outside, happening simultaneously. Dorothy, trim and always chic, be it in the latest swimwear or in a luncheon suit, dated the most eligible bachelors and began a romantic involvement with the producer Felix Young. (Finally, she had legally ended her marriage to Jack Wiener.)

It was only a matter of time before the Fields children (particularly Herb) convinced Lew and Rose to leave New York and come west; no small feat. But the elder Fieldses were beginning to feel their age and the loneliness of retirement, being separated from their children and the accustomed hive of activity. So they sold their Chappaqua, New York, country estate, auctioned off the contents they didn't want to move, and joined the young Fieldses in their house on Rodeo Drive. If Lew needed more convincing that he was doing the right thing, it came with the notion that out there he would be in line for any work the studios might be offering. (In fact, Lew Fields did make some appearances in films, notably playing himself in the Astaire-Rogers *The Story of Vernon and Irene Castle*, and in the biopic *Lillian Russell*, with Alice Faye.) For Lew and Rose, the family's living all together again was like old times, but roomier. The main difference was that for the first time in their lives, Joe, Herb, and Dorothy saw their father around the house. Rose once more ruled the domain and restored the tradition of Sunday dinner, which was often the only time everyone saw one another. The rest of the week, life was such a party atmosphere that rather than keep food around, someone would pick up the phone and order out from the local market from meal to meal. Lew surrounded himself with old theatre cronies like Willie Collier, Marie Dressler, and Joe Weber, who'd also come west. Dressed as dapperly as always, he still frequented the racetrack, bankrolled now by Dorothy and Herb, who also supplied their parents with an allowance. Lew was still such a respected and famous man that when he entered one of his favorite haunts like the Brown Derby, people would applaud. Almost everybody, including his children's star pals like the Gershwins, Fred Astaire, and Cole Porter, called him Mr. Fields.

The three Fields children had always been on a constant quest to win their father's approval, but Dorothy now seemed to be the one with the achievements to make him most proud; ironic, since he had bitterly opposed her entry into show business in the first place, whether in having her ejected from publishers' offices or confiscating her acceptance letter for summer stock work. (By the time his children's generation had come of age, of course, show business had not only lost its disreputable connotation, it had become a glamorous public aspiration.)

Dorothy's success with the studio continued to increase. When she and McHugh returned to New York for Lew's *Vanderbilt Revue* in 1930, they'd written ten songs for MGM. They'd added to their run of Broadway-originating hit songs a few the studio could take credit for: "Go Home and Tell Your Mother" and, the following year, "Cuban Love Song." (The same year, 1931, one of their two *Singin' the Blues* songs, "It's the Darndest Thing," also became a hit.) In the meantime, the team also supplied a couple of songs, neither of them memorable, to the film version of De Sylva, Brown, and Henderson's successful Broadway vehicle for Bert Lahr, *Flying High*.

When Dorothy and McHugh returned to New York in 1932, it was to perform on the opening night bill of that mammoth and spectacular symbol of the movie palace, Radio City Music Hall, which had just been completed. Built by the Rockefellers and S. L. "Roxy" Rothafel, it was the largest and most expensive music hall in the world, with a stage (also the largest anywhere) 144 feet wide and 80 feet deep, and a curtain lifted by thirteen motors. The equally lavish interior with its towering chandelier and red and gold art deco glory had been Roxy's vision. (After the opening gala, by the way, the movie chosen to christen the place was Frank Capra's *The Bitter Tea of General Yen*, with Barbara Stanwyck as an American missionary who falls in love with a Chinese warlord.)

Opening night, two days after Christmas, was a madhouse outside (with 700 extra policemen brought in for crowd control). Celebrities and other important luminaries filled the 6,200 seats. John D. Rockefeller, Jr., was there with his son Nelson, as were

RADIO - KEITH - ORPHEUM
PROUDLY PRESENTS
THE INAUGURAL PROGRAM
OF THE
RADIO CITY MUSIC HALL
UNDER THE PERSONAL DIRECTION OF

Roxy

RADIO CITY
IN ROCKEFELLER CENTER
•

Gene Tunney, Irving Berlin and his wife, Ellin, RCA/NBC founder David Sarnoff (whose headquarters location would supply the "Radio" in Radio City), Leopold Stokowski, Alfred Smith, and Amelia Earhart. The national news media, including radio, were there in force, as they had been in chronicling the excitement leading up to the event.

Dorothy, now twenty-seven, and Jimmy McHugh had been asked to write two songs for the occasion, and to perform them onstage personally—the only songwriters so honored. Lew and Joe Weber were to appear as part of the minstrel show finale. The rest of the evening's entertainment was a variety grab bag of star talent drawn from every corner of the performing arts that made for an eclectic show (and a really long one—the finale didn't begin till half past midnight. Dorothy later remarked, "It went on forever. I remember Peggy Fears commented it was the first time she ever saw 3,000 people sleeping together").

The Roxyettes were the forerunners of . . . . (Yes.) Dorothy got up to sing the two songs "With a Feather in Your Cap" and the optimistic "Hey Young Fella (Close Your Old Umbrella)" with McHugh at the piano. The first was a production number, the second, a nightclub sketch. And though she admitted to being nervous beforehand, she stepped up confidently to the microphone and put across her own lyrics like a seasoned pro—even though she hadn't performed onstage since her amateur show days with Rodgers and Hart and at the Benjamin School. *Variety* commented that she and McHugh did better than "others on the bill who do nothing else but appear on stages." (Dorothy had long since given up her stage ambitions, and unlike Johnny Mercer or Comden and Green, she wasn't a lyricist/performer. On the other hand, she and McHugh did make occasional radio appearances to sing their songs, and throughout her career, she was known to get up at one event or another to show off her work, as she did for private parties.)

Program for the 1932 opening night of the newly built Radio City Music Hall. Inside it points out: "Miss Fields, daughter of Lew Fields, is making her first stage appearance."

HAPPY NEW YEAR

•

THE PROGRAM

•

The Entire Performance Conceived and Supervised by "ROXY,"
Director-General of the Radio City Music Hall and the RKO Roxy Theatre

1. MINSTRELSY

DE WOLF HOPPER, THE TUSKEGEE CHOIR, TH
RADIO CITY MUSIC HALL BALLET AND CHORU

2. THE RADIO CITY MUSIC HALL ROXYETTES

Directed by Russell Markert

3. WEBER AND FIELDS

4. VERA SCHWARZ *of the Staats-Oper, Berlin*

Who is making her first appearance in America at th
invitation of "Roxy"
"LIEBESWALZER," from "Wiener Blut," *Johann Strau*
Specially arranged by Leo Blech

5. BERRY BROTHERS, *Dancers*

6. IMPRESSIONS OF A MUSIC HALL

(A) THE WALLENDAS, *Continental Aerialists*
(B) THE KIKUTAS, *Oriental Risley Act*

7. IN THE SPOTLIGHT

EDDIE AND RALPH

8. HARALD KREUTZBERG

Assisted by Margaret Sande, The Radio City Ballet Corp
and Male Dancers, presenting, for the first time anywher
"THE ANGEL OF FATE," *A Dramatic Dance Scen*
Choreography by Harald Kreutzberg. Music by Friedrich Wilcker
The Angel of Fate, descending from Heaven to perform his wor
on earth, visits a royal feast. Displeased at the orgy, he places th
Mask of Death upon the King's face. Later, meeting an innocen
maiden, the Angel finds, to his sorrow, that she becomes sophist
cated through his teaching, and too becomes a victim of the Deat
Mask. On a battlefield the Angel dances with a mask symbolic o
modern warfare. The soldiers, following the Angel's example, lif
their masks to their faces, and die. In the final scene, the Ange
his tasks on earth completed, ascends once more to Heaven.

9. RAY BOLGER, *outstanding young American Dancing Comedia*

10. THE TUSKEGEE CHOIR . William L. Dawson, *Directo*

(A) "Beautiful City" . . . . . *William L. Dawso*
(B) "Hospodi Pomilui" . . . . *Lvovsk*
(Male Chorus)
(C) "Good News" (traditional) *Arr. by William L. Dawso*
This is the first appearance of this celebrated choral organization i
New York, who come from Tuskegee Institute specially for th
engagement.

11. THE RADIO CITY MUSIC HALL BALLET

PATRICIA BOWMAN, *Premiere Danseuse*
Choreography by Florence Rogge.   Music by Maurice Bar

12. DOCTOR ROCKWELL

13. NIGHT CLUB REVELS

RAY BOLGER, BERRY BROS., JULES AND JOSIE WALTON,
DOROTHY FIELDS, JIMMY McHUGH, GERTRUDE NIESEN,
THE RADIO CITY ROXYETTES, AND THE BALLET CORPS
(Miss Fields, daughter of Lew Fields, is making her first stage appearance)
THE RADIO CITY MUSIC HALL ROXYETTES, BALLET CORPS, CHORUS
"MAD MOMENTS" . . . . by Harry Revel and Mack Gordon
"HEY, YOUNG FELLA!" by Dorothy Fields and Jimmy McHugh

I had nothing to sing about, the days were cloudy and wet.
Had no sunshine to fling about and lots of rain to forget.
Wore my flannels and stayed indoors, like a bird in a tree,
How I shivered and prayed indoors, 'till one day you yelled to me—

CHORUS

Hey! Young Fella, will you close ya old umbrella,
Have a glorious day throwing rubbers away,
'Cause it ain't gonna rain no more.
Say, Young Fella, put your raincoat in the cellar,
While you're tying your tie, taka peak at the sky;
Well, it ain't gonna rain no more!
Look at the brave little rainbow fighting those clouds up above.
I'm in the ring, Mister Rainbow, with a horseshoe in my glove.
Hey, Young Fella, better close your old umbrella,
Give your trousers a hitch 'cause ya gonna be rich
And it ain't gonna rain no more.

INTERMISSION

14. EXCERPTS FROM "CARMEN" . . . . . *Bizet*

Carmen . . . . COE GLADE
Escamillo . . . . DESIRE DEFRERE
Don Jose . . . . AROLDO LINDI
The Dancer . . . . . PATRICIA BOWMAN
The Radio City Music Hall Chorus, Ballet, Roxyettes, soldiers,
matadors, cigarette girls, etc.
1. Street Scene
2. Cigarette Song
3. In the Tavern
4. The Flower Song
5. At the Mountain Pass
6. Orchestral Interlude
7. Plaza del Toro
Directed by Desiré Defrere, formerly stage director of the Chicago
Civic Opera. Choreography by Florence Rogge.

15. BARTO AND MANN

16. THE RADIO CITY MUSIC HALL ROXYETTES

Directed by RUSSELL MARKERT
"WITH A FEATHER IN YOUR CAP"
Music by Jimmy McHugh.   Lyric by Dorothy Fields.
GERTRUDE NIESEN, Soloist

17. "SEPT. 13, 1814" . . . . *Arranged by* FERDE GROFE

Francis Scott Key . . . . . TAYLOR HOLMES
THE RADIO CITY MUSIC HALL MALE ENSEMBLE
On the night of Sept. 13, 1814, a young American, Francis Scott
Key, was a prisoner-of-war on a British frigate during the bombard-
ment of Fort McHenry. During the action, pictured in this scene,
young Key received the inspiration for that noble poem that later
became our National Anthem.

CURTAIN

(NOTE: Every effort will be made to adhere to the program
outlined above, but it is subject to alteration or change of routine.)

THE RADIO CITY THEATRES
PRODUCTION STAFF

Production Director . . . . Leon Leonidoff
Art Director . . . . Robert Edmond Jones
Musical Director . . . . Erno Rapee
Associate Conductors—Charles Previn, Joseph Littau, Macklin Morrow,
Leonid Leonardi
Staff Composers and Arrangers—Ferde Grofe, Maurice Baron, Desidir
D'Antalffy, Earle Moss, Otto Cesana
Staff Organists—Dick Leibert, C. A. J. Parmentier, Betty Gould
Associate Art Director . . . . James Reynolds
Ballet Director . . . . Florence Rogge
Director of Opera . . . . Desiré Defrere
Associate Ballet-Master . . . . Lasar Galpern
Director of Roxyettes . . . . Russell Markert
Director of Chorus . . . . Leon Rosebrook
Associate Chorus Director . . . . . . Max Herzberg
Director of Radio Programs . . . . . Leo Russotto
Master of Effects . . . . Max Manne
Stage Director . . . . William Stern
Electrical Engineer . . . . Eugene Braun
Chief Sound Engineer . . . . Harry Hiller
Chief Projectionist . . . . Arthur Smith
In Charge of Costumes . . . . Hattie Rogge

ADMINISTRATIVE STAFF

Chief of Administration . . . . James H. Turner
Assistant to "Roxy" . . . . S. Jay Kaufman
Manager of Theatres . . . . Charles W. Griswold
Director of Publicity . . . . . . Martha L. Wilchinski
Secretary to "Roxy" . . . . Leah Klar
In Charge of Maintenance . . . . . David P. Canavan
Supervisor of Hospitals . . . . . . Anne Beckerle, R. N.

The Contour Curtain constructed under the Ted Weidhaas patents
by Peter Clark, Inc.
Musical instruments in the Night Club scene supplied through
the courtesy of The Conn Musical Instrument Company. Motion
picture scenic effects in Technicolor by Robert Bruce. Lobby and
photographic display under direction of M. M. Geffen.

RADIO
CITY
MUSIC
HALL

FIFTIETH STRE
AND SIXTH AV
NEW YORK

TWO PERFORMANC
DAILY..2:15..8:15 P.

MGM was glad to see Fields and McHugh back in Hollywood. They supplied the nonmusical picture *Dinner at Eight* with its title song. (Based on George S. Kaufman and Edna Ferber's play, it had an all-star cast led by John Barrymore and is probably best remembered for the exchange between Marie Dressler and Jean Harlow in which the latter marvels at reading that machinery is going to take the place of every profession; Dressler replies, "That's something *you* need *never* worry about.")

While the song "Dinner at Eight" was a notable success of 1933, "Don't Blame Me," picked up by Hollywood from Lew Leslie's *Clowns in Clover* and reassigned to MGM's *Meet the Baron*, became one of the year's top hits and one of the team's most enduring standards. Their "Hey Young Fella (Close Your Old Umbrella" also shared the top of the charts that year with "Carioca," "Easter Parade," "Flying Down to Rio," "Heat Wave," "It's Only a Paper Moon," "Let's Fall in Love," "Lover," "Smoke Gets in Your Eyes," "Sophisticated Lady," "Stormy Weather," "We're in the Money," and "Who's Afraid of the Big Bad Wolf."

The last is interesting because "Who's Afraid of the Big Bad Wolf," written for the Disney animated short *The Three Little Pigs*, not only became a popular Depression anthem, but was penned by Ann Ronnell, one of the few other women songwriters active in '30s Hollywood.

It wasn't that Dorothy had a stranglehold on women's contributions to the mainstream songbook of the time—quite. Ronnell, for instance, had already had a hit the previous year with "Willow Weep for Me" (recorded by Paul Whiteman and his orchestra, with Irene Taylor) and would coauthor "Linda," with Jack Lawrence (fifteen years later), which was the extent of her notable songs.

There were other women, too: Kay Swift wrote the music for the songs "Can This Be Love" and "Fine and Dandy" for a 1930 show of the latter name (she collaborated with her husband, banker James P. Warburg, who wrote as Paul James). The year before,

eet music for the title song of MGM's *Dinner at Eight* starring John Barrymore and Jean Harlow, ong others

APPEARING FIRST IN A REVUE CALLED

Clowns in Clover in 1933, "Don't Blame Me" is one of the best known Fields and McHugh ballads. McHugh's straightforward melody is set off by Dorothy's lyric, which exhibits her penchant for casual internal rhyme, as in the first and second lines of the verse, and also "spell" and "help," repeating the word "do," "conceal" and "feeling," "moon" and "you," and so on. It all carries the lyric forward in an easy flow that is one of the trademarks of a Dorothy Fields lyric. "Don't Blame Me" was recorded by Ethel Waters, Guy Lombardo and his Royal Canadians, and in 1948 was revived by Nat "King" Cole.

Dorothy's craftsmanship was impeccable. In the days before rock and roll and contemporary pop slackened things to the point where words like "mind" and "time" are acceptable rhymes, the craftsmanship of a lyric was of the utmost importance. Elements like the quality and placement of rhymes, stresses, vowels, the relationship of the word to the note values—all these were labored over by lyricists like Oscar Hammerstein, who sometimes took three weeks to write a lyric, and Ira Gershwin, who was nicknamed "The Jeweler."

Which is why "A Fine Romance," for instance, is even more fun, because Dorothy wrote it so the prosody—the stress on the syllables in ROmance—is wrong; the irony is increased by the disgust the pronunciation of the word adds to the song.

Dorothy with Jimmy McHugh
before one of their radio
appearances

DON'T BLAME ME

Ever since the lucky night I
found you
I've hung around you, just like a
fool
Falling head and heels in love
Like a kid out of school.

My poor heart is in an awful state
now
But it's too late now to call a halt
So if I become a nuisance
It's all your fault!

Don't blame me
For falling in love with you
I'm under your spell but how can
I help it,
Don't blame me!

Can't you see
When you do the things you do,
If I can't conceal the thrill that I'm
feeling
Don't blame me.

I can't help it if that doggoned
moon above
Makes me need someone like
you to love!

Blame your kiss,
As sweet as a kiss can be
And blame all your charms, that
melt in my arms
But don't blame me.

they'd written "Can't We Be Friends?," which was a top hit of 1929 and became Swift's only standard.

Then there was Doris Fisher in the mid-1940s, writing words and music with Allan Roberts in Hollywood. They had about eight notable songs, particularly "Put the Blame on Mame" (they were put to work at Columbia writing for Rita Hayworth movies), "You Always Hurt the One You Love," "Into Each Life Some Rain Must Fall," "Prove It by the Things You Do (It's Easy to Say)," and "Tired" (popularized by Pearl Bailey).

Other women, such as Sylvia Fine (writing for her husband, Danny Kaye) and Kay Thompson, were writing some comedy and special material. But though witty and brilliant, no examples attained the mainstream or lasting visibility of comic classics like Noël Coward's "Don't Put Your Daughter on the Stage."

A generation before hers, Dorothy had two predecessors. One was Dorothy Donnelly, who wrote lyrics and librettos with Sigmund Romberg, most notably for 1924's *The Student Prince* with its memorable stalwarts "The Drinking Song" and "Deep in My Heart, Dear." Other collaborations with Romberg included *Blossom Time* and *My Maryland*. Fields also had a predecessor in her coed partnership with Jerome Kern: Anne Caldwell, who wrote lyrics in the late 'teens and early '20s for Kern shows like *The Stepping Stones* ("Raggedy Ann"), *Good Morning, Dearie* ("Ka-Lu-A"), and *The Night Boat* ("Whose Baby Are You"). Caldwell's lyrics were hailed as pleasant but unremarkable at the time and the songs don't survive as standards. Caldwell and Donnelly, though, represented the small group of "lady writers" who wrote in the early part of the century for musical theatre—or more precisely, for operetta. Operetta, of course, unlike vaudeville- and jazz-tainted musical comedy, was civilized, ennobled, had family values. Most important, all that purity and romanticism was ladylike.

Only a decade later, Dorothy was Kern's second woman collaborator, but the jazz-age, liberated Fields was a generation and a universe away from Caldwell. For though Dorothy's work was imbued with a distinctly feminine take on life, it was as bold and edgy as the work of any of her leading male contemporaries. It was generally too ironic and dead-on to exude any of the "old-fashioned-female" qualities like sentimentality, coyness, or self-sacrificing nobility that were negatively associated with "women's" creations, be it Caldwell's girly style or in Fannie Hurst's tearjerking novels *Back Street* and *Imitation of Life*.

In the mid-1940s Betty Comden would come along. Of the generation following Dorothy's, Comden was perhaps closest in spirit to her work and career, writing with Adolph Green the lyrics for standards like "The Party's Over," "Make Someone Happy," "Lucky to Be Me," and "New York, New York"—also demonstrating her great skill as a librettist. On the other hand, not only is it impossible to extricate Comden's voice from that of her co-lyricist, Adolph Green, but with the exception of the aforementioned and a few others, the Comden and Green songs were so rooted in their musical theatre contexts that they are seldom performed outside the shows for which they were written.

In actuality, Dorothy's position as the lone woman heavyweight in the business didn't seem to affect her or any of her male colleagues in 1930s Hollywood (just as it had made few blink on Broadway). Had she been a studio executive or a director, forced to battle her way through the male hierarchy with confrontation and power struggles, it would obviously have been a different matter. As it was, Dorothy did purely creative work and was universally respected as a topflight professional. Her collaborators, while the first to recognize *la différence*, didn't stop to think much beyond that. Musicians and other artists tend (more than the general population) to have higher tolerance, anyway, regarding things like the race and sex barriers that hang up the rest of society, if they're impressed by talent. In any case, it would have been hard for "the boys" to argue with Dorothy's track record and facility, even if this colleague was a manicured lady who continually filled her house with flowers.

Work still meant getting together with Jimmy McHugh— either around his piano or hers or in their office on the MGM back lot. But Dorothy started to get occasional assignments with other

Dorothy, turned out with requisite suit and hat, in 1935—a year in which she provided scores for some five different movies

composers. Among the slew of movies to which she contributed in the early and mid-thirties were RKO's *Alice Adams*, the 1935 Katharine Hepburn vehicle, for which Dorothy wrote a song called "I Can't Waltz Alone," with music by film score deity Max Steiner; *In Person* (again at RKO), Ginger Rogers's first starring vehicle, with songs by Dorothy and actor-pianist-comedian-composer Oscar Levant (songs included "Out of Sight, Out of Mind," "Got a New Lease on Life," and "Don't Mention Love to Me"). With McHugh, there was *Dancing Lady* (Joan Crawford and Clark Gable), to which they contributed the title song, although in addition to songs by

Rodgers and Hart, the hit was scored by Burton Lane and Harold Adamson with their "Everything I Have Is Yours"; *Meet the Baron*, with Jack Pearl, Jimmy Durante, and Zasu Pitts; director George Stevens's *The Nitwits*; and *The Prizefighter and the Lady*, which starred Myrna Loy with boxer Max Baer (Dorothy would later write Baer's nightclub act). On loan to RKO in 1935, they did *Hooray for Love,* with Ann Sothern and Bill Robinson (also appearing, Fats Waller), and had a top hit with the title song. For Paramount and *Every Night at Eight* (which starred George Raft with Alice Faye, Frances Langford, and Patsy Kelly as a radio sister act), Fields and

Bill "Bojangles" Robinson in *Hooray for Love* (which also starred Ann Sothern), 1935. Robinson had starred in Fields and McHugh's *Blackbirds of 1928*.

PARAMOUNT'S

Every Night at Eight was a show business romantic comedy that starred tough guy George Raft, with Alice Faye, Frances Langford, and Patsy Kelly as singing radio sisters. *Variety* succinctly dismissed the movie as "another case of missed opportunity." But two of its songs (the ones beginning in the first person singular) would outshine the vehicle: "I'm in the Mood for Love" and "I Feel a Song Comin' On." "I Feel a Song Comin' On" was sung in the film by Harry Barris and reprised by Faye, Langford, and Kelly; it was Langford who popularized it.

The other song would turn out to be perhaps Fields and McHugh's most renowned ballad. "I'm in the Mood for Love" was sung by Langford, and when recorded by Little Jack Little and his Orchestra, promptly became a Number One chart record. A cover (competing) record was made by Louis Armstrong, and the song was revived by Billy Eckstine in 1946. Recorded by countless others, today it remains a staple of every chanteuse's repertoire.

Every Night at Eight, 1935. L to r: George Raft, Frances Langford, Alice Faye, and Patsy Kelly and their sombreros

I FEEL A SONG COMIN' ON

I feel a song comin' on
And I'm warning ya,
It's a victorious,
Happy and glorious new strain!

I feel a song comin' on
It's a melody
Full of the laughter
Of children out after the rain.

You'll hear a tuneful story
Ringin' through ya.
Love and glory! Hallelujah!

And now that my troubles are
    gone
Let those heavenly
Drums go drummin', cause
I feel a song comin' on!

"WE HAD AN APARTMENT ON GRACIE SQUARE,"

says Irving Berlin's eldest daughter, Mary Ellin Barrett, "and we used to have Christmas parties. And what's vivid in my mind is this view of Dorothy at the piano. It was either 1944 or 1945, and sometime during this convivial evening, someone asked Dorothy to sit down and play some songs—which she did. And what impressed me was what a wonderful, solid pianist she was—just a simple, direct, swinging pop piano. What surprised me was that the lyricist would be such a great piano player. And what I also remember is her singing 'I'm in the Mood for Love'—not in a memorable voice, but one of those songwriter voices that's just right for the song. Just the savviest lady at the piano."

I'M IN THE MOOD FOR LOVE

Lovely interlude!
Most romantic mood
And your attitude is right, dear.
Sweetheart, you have me under
     a spell!
Now my dream is real
That is why I feel
Such a strong appeal tonight.
Somehow all my reason takes
     flight, dear

I'm in the mood for love
Simply because you're near me;
Funny, but when you're near me
I'm in the mood for love.

Heaven is in your eyes
Bright as the stars we're under;
Oh, is it any wonder
I'm in the mood for love?

Why stop to think of whether
This little dream might fade?
We've put our hearts together
Now we are one, I'm not afraid.

If there's a cloud above,
If it should rain we'll let it.
But for tonight, forget it!
I'm in the mood for love.

Joan Crawford in her
pre–Mildred Pierce period.
Dancing Lady, 1933.

McHugh contributed what would be two of their biggest hits: "I Feel a Song Comin' On" and the perennial ballad "I'm in the Mood for Love"—both hits of 1935 (with "I'm in the Mood for Love" ranked number five in "Your Hit Parade"'s first year).

Nineteen-thirty-five was a watershed year for Dorothy in Hollywood. Not only did she work on eight movies, including the six mentioned above, and have six hit songs, most important, three of her hits of the year were "Lovely to Look At," "I Won't Dance," and "I Dream Too Much"—none of them written with Jimmy McHugh. Instead, they were the first fruits of her almost accidental collaboration with her idol, Jerome Kern, with whom her future lay. Dorothy was rapidly heading for an Oscar. When she finally got it, it was not McHugh who was beside her, but Kern.

Henry Fonda and Lily Pons in *I Dream Too Much*

BACK IN 1904 Lew Fields had given the young composer Jerome Kern one of his first breaks when he bought an early effort of Kern's for his show *An English Daisy*. In the next couple of decades, through the series of musicals he wrote for the Princess Theatre with Guy Bolton and P. G. Wodehouse, Kern was held largely responsible for transforming the American musical from lavish extravaganzas (like the ones Lew Fields produced) to intimate, smart, contemporary musical comedies. The Princess Theatre shows galvanized a generation of juvenile theatregoers like the Gershwins, Rodgers and Hart, and Herb and Dorothy Fields—who would, under the Princess shows' influence, bring their own changes to the form in the 1920s.

To the generation of songwriters who came of age in the '20s and '30s, Jerome Kern was God. He was referred to in those circles as "The Dean," but "God" was really what they meant. He inspired a fair amount of intimidation along with immense awe, and virtually always got his own way in whatever creative or business dealing he was engaged. For one thing, he pointedly only worked with people he liked.

After Bolton and Wodehouse, and alternately with Otto Harbach, the young Oscar Hammerstein II had been Kern's major collaborator in the '20s and early '30s (the studious Harbach had been Hammerstein's mentor, and had brought him to Kern). Together, Hammerstein and Kern had changed the course of musical theatre with *Show Boat*. Hammerstein's vision of a musical with a fully integrated score that advanced the narrative and characterization of a dramatically meaningful book brought *Show Boat* into the world in 1927. Musicals would never be quite the same, though the show stood by itself for years until the early 1940s, when, after *Pal Joey* (book by John O'Hara), Rodgers and Hammerstein continued the redefinition of the musical play with *Oklahoma!*

Two theatrical events occurred in the early '30s that precipitated Kern's relationship with Dorothy Fields. First, there was Kern and Harbach's *Roberta*, which, despite a talented cast that included the young Bob Hope, George Murphy, Ray Middleton, and veteran Fay Templeton, almost flopped in the wake of a divided press. (Fred MacMurray was one of "The California Collegians" also appearing in the show.) It finally caught on and ran 295 performances pro- pelled by the popularity of "Smoke Gets in Your Eyes." The follow- ing year, Kern and Hammerstein opened their new show, *Three Sisters*, in London, where it met with resounding (and humiliating) failure. The combination of *Roberta*'s close shave and the *Three Sisters* disaster sent Kern off to Hollywood for permanent peace and security. Hammerstein followed, and they continued to collaborate.

Roberta had been bought by RKO and its bright, energetic head of production, twenty-nine-year-old Pandro Berman, who saw it as a vehicle for Fred Astaire and Ginger Rogers. Randolph Scott would play the halfback who inherits his aunt's Paris dress salon. And for the starring role of the Russian princess-turned-dressmaker who accompanies herself on the guitar, Irene Dunne was brought in.

Kern attended to his duties surrounding the transfer of *Roberta* to film, and then he headed on a trip east. The story goes that he'd written a sixteen-bar melody for which the studio decided they needed words; Pandro Berman called in Dorothy Fields. Dorothy was in the midst of her busiest and most successful year in Hollywood to date, and had been doing some work for Berman and RKO.

Kern's sixteen-bar melody created an odd situation. The stan- dard form for a popular song was thirty-two bars—usually an AABA form, where an eight-bar theme was repeated, a different theme (or release) was presented for another eight bars, and then a return to the original theme. This one defied convention. When asked later why he wrote it in only sixteen bars, Kern replied: "That was all I had to say."

Adding to the challenge, Berman told Dorothy they needed the song to be used both for a fashion show and as a love song. Dorothy took the melody away from their meeting and the next day came back with the completed lyric for "Lovely to Look At." To Dorothy's distress, Berman proceeded to take the lyric and shoot the entire scene without the Dean's approval—of Dorothy, the lyric, the scene—anything. That wasn't how one operated with Kern, and if one did, there was usually vituperative hell to pay. Dorothy was all the more anxious about the outcome because Kern had been her idol since childhood. But although he was a friend of Lew's, knew Rose and also Herb, Dorothy didn't know him at all. However, Berman reassured her, and luckily for the production, when Kern was shown the footage, he loved it, and was mightily impressed by Dorothy's effort.

There would be another job for Dorothy on *Roberta*. "I Won't Dance" was originally the only catchy number from the ill-fated Kern-Hammerstein collaboration *Three Sisters*. Fred Astaire, who'd seen the show in London, suggested the song be bought for use in *Roberta*. When the studio wanted different, "jazzier" lyrics, Dorothy was again tapped. It was only with *Roberta* and the Fields version that "I Won't Dance" finally became a hit, as did "Lovely to Look At."

To Kern's mind, he had found a new partner. Hammerstein was increasingly disgusted with Hollywood, and began turning his attentions back toward New York. His luck hadn't been as good as it once had been and would be again soon (though there was some notable work, like putting *Show Boat* on film). Kern and Dorothy hit it off instantly, immediately developing a rapport and deep personal affection that would last until the day Kern died.

It was the kind of relationship she had never developed with Jimmy McHugh. Nobody remembers ever hearing an angry word or raised voice between Fields and McHugh; McHugh's son would later recall their always relating as "a lady and a gentleman." But their personal chemistry never clicked the way their songs did. There had forever been a politeness, a formality, a distance between them, and finally, it seemed, they just began to get on each other's

THE COPYRIGHT AND OTHER DOCUMENTATION

list Jimmy McHugh as co-lyricist (and thus the third author) of "Lovely to Look At." Actually, it was the nature of the contract between Fields and McHugh that kept them a team on paper even as they were beginning to work with other people. (In similar arrangements, not at all uncommon in those days, film composer Herbert Stothart is listed as coauthor on "Cuban Love Song" and McHugh and Otto Harbach on Jerome Kern and Oscar Hammerstein/Dorothy Fields's "I Won't Dance.")

"Lovely to Look At" was definitely the beginning of the end of her partnership with McHugh. Having set Kern's sixteen-bar melody in his absence, when they finally did meet, Dorothy and American popular music's elder statesman were struck with instant affection for each other, and quickly developed a harmonious working relationship, in spite of the delight Kern took in riling people, particularly women, just to get a reaction. Introduced in *Roberta* by Kern favorite Irene Dunne, "Lovely to Look At" was recorded by Eddy Duchin and his Orchestra and became a Number One chart record.

Lovely to look at. The fashion show from *Roberta*, in the salon of Irene Dunne—
which brought together the talents of Dorothy Fields and Jerome Kern

LOVELY TO LOOK AT

Clothes must play a part
To light an eye, to win a heart;
They say a gown can almost
    speak,
If it is chic.
Should you select the right
    effect, you cannot miss,
You may be sure, he will tell you
    this

Lovely to look at,
Delightful to know and heaven to
    kiss.

A combination like this,
Is quite my most impossible
    scheme come true,
Imagine finding a dream like
    you!

You're lovely to look at,
It's thrilling to hold you terribly
    tight.
For we're together, the moon is
    new,
And oh, it's lovely to look at you
    tonight!

ALTHOUGH THE ORIGINAL BROADWAY VERSION

of *Roberta* contained songs like "Yesterdays," "Let's Begin," and "Smoke Gets in Your Eyes" (with Otto Harbach's lyrics to Kern's music), "I Won't Dance" was not among them. Actually, it had been written by Kern and Oscar Hammerstein for their 1935 show, *Three Sisters*, set in World War I-era Britain, which had opened in London to a short and painful run. It was Fred Astaire who'd suggested the song go into the filmed *Roberta* (1935), with new lyrics by Dorothy. The Hammerstein version of "I Won't Dance" is occasionally performed today; with its charm, it's unfortunate that more people aren't familiar with it.

But Dorothy's snappy translation of Hammerstein's conceit (as performed in the movie by Astaire and Ginger Rogers) suddenly became a hit. Recorded by Eddy Duchin and his Orchestra, it reached Number One on the charts.

Randolph Scott stuck in an elevator
in the House of Roberta, as Irene
Dunne looks concerned

I WON'T DANCE

Think of what you're losing
By constantly refusing to dance
   with me.
You'd be the idol of France
   with me!
And yet you stand there and
   shake your foolish head dra-
   matically
While I wait here so ecstatically
And you just look and say
   emphatically
Not this season!
There's a reason!

I won't dance! don't ask me;
I won't dance! don't ask me;
I won't dance, madame, with
   you.
My heart won't let my feet do
   things they should do!

You know what? You're lovely,
And so what? You're lovely!

But oh, what you do to me!
I'm like an ocean wave that's
   bumped on the shore;
I feel so absolutely stumped on
   the floor!

When you dance you're charm-
   ing and you're gentle!
'Specially when you do the
   "Continental"
But this feeling isn't purely
   mental;
For heaven rest us,
I'm not asbestos.
And that's why

I won't dance! Why should I?
I won't dance! How could I?
I won't dance! *Merci beaucoup*!
I know that music leads the way
   to romance:
So if I hold you in my arms
I won't dance!

nerves. They quietly moved on, beginning around the time Dorothy began
her relationship with Kern. McHugh
would have a long and successful
career working with a variety of other
lyricists, particularly Harold
Adamson, with whom he had hits
like "It's a Most Unusual Day," "A
Lovely Way to Spend an
Evening," "Where Are You?," and
the Nat "King" Cole hit "Too Young
to Go Steady." McHugh and Dorothy continued
to remain on amiable terms.

If Fields and McHugh were a rather unlikely couple, Fields
and Kern were an even odder one. Dorothy at 5' 5½" towered over
the unstatuesque maestro, who was nineteen years her senior. As no
one else would dare, she called him "Junior." And he let her. She
immediately became a member of the Kern family, which was centered at the Beverly-Wilshire Hotel until a home (designed to be a
replica of the French Provincial family home in Bronxville, New
York) was eventually built on Whittier Drive in Beverly Hills.

Kern's commanding manner was only one facet of the man's
personality. He'd had a privileged early life, born on Manhattan's
fashionable Sutton Place into a wealthy and cultivated German-
Jewish family. He was a connoisseur and avid collector of antiques,
with a perfect eye. In fact, he aided and supported Dorothy
Hammerstein in setting up her Beverly Hills decorating business.
(She'd eventually decorate not only Norma Talmadge's and Pandro
Berman's houses, but Dorothy Fields's as well.)

Kern also had a pixieish side, which focused on two things. He
loved to argue, and took pleasure in starting terrific fights at dinner
parties and other social functions, just for the bracing rush of caus-
ing havoc. Also, he was an incessant and enthusiastic practical joker.
One occasion had him, while in London, wondering whether he
could singlehandedly shut down a construction site. He then stood
around long enough for people to infer that he was the owner, com-
plimented the foreman on the wonderful job everyone was doing,
and proceeded to dismiss the entire crew for the day. Another time,
he let a herd of sheep loose on the property of a friend who wouldn't

cut his lawn. At the Beverly-Wilshire, he enjoyed stopping traffic by stepping out onto his balcony to carry on Mussolini-style.

Kern was also deeply emotional, not shy about showing temper, and utterly devoted to his music. He suffered his first heart attack when his treasured Bluthner grand piano was delivered from New York, and as it was unpacked he realized that the movers had inadvertently screwed down the packing case right through the piano's sounding board. His heart attack almost immediately afterward was followed by a stroke several days later. (He would recover fairly well from both. His piano, however, even after repair, would never sound quite the same to him.)

Once work had been completed on *Roberta*, RKO signed Kern to write a vehicle for Metropolitan Opera star Lily Pons called *I Dream Too Much*. Kern specified that Dorothy was to be his lyricist, and arranged with Pandro Berman for her to get a contract for $1,000 a week (he was getting $5,000). Part of Dorothy still couldn't believe that she was working with her idol, but she quickly put that aside as they settled into a routine. As with Jimmy McHugh and every other composer she worked with, the melody always came first. With Kern, she would take home a lead sheet, write and rewrite at home, and come in the next day prepared. Then around the piano, they'd continue to work on it. On top of the piano Kern always kept a basket of pencils and a small bust of Wagner, which he'd use as a barometer of the work they were doing. If Kern played something and thought he picked up on a reaction on his companion's face that was less than ecstatic, or if he wasn't happy with something himself, he would turn the bust to face the other way and say, "Wagner doesn't like that." If he was pleased, he would give what Dorothy called "that wonderful shake of his head."

She learned an enormous amount from Kern, who was arguably the greatest melodist American music ever produced (he would pass the torch to Richard Rodgers). "Kern had this lyric simplicity of melody," Dorothy would say later, "this direct, straight musical line." One thing Dorothy became more conscious of was how to place vowels and consonants. Kern's melodies were, in the truest sense, written to be sung, and he was especially particular that the lyric should accommodate the singer as well—for instance, coupling high notes with open vowels.

Kern loved Dorothy, and they forged a relationship of warm and deep affection. He loved her brightness and humor, and how the house filled with laughter when she was around. He was a martinet and intimidated people, but not her. While she respected and certainly didn't want to cross him, she saw through his bravado, and regarded him as cute; he in turn, admired her talent and looked on her with amusement.

Kern liked to work at night, and when they weren't working, Dorothy was hanging around the household. She came early in the day and stayed late, spending a lot of time with Kern's teenaged daughter, Betty. Kern and his daughter were especially close and devoted to each other. Kern's wife, Eva, who was British, was more distant, and mother and daughter never got on particularly well. For Betty, Dorothy was like an older sister, or aunt, who would sit with her for hours by the pool, just talking and offering a compassionate ear to her growing pains. More than fifty years later, Betty (who eventually married Artie Shaw) would remember that Dorothy "lit up her life" whenever she came in. (In fact, Dorothy enjoyed spending time with children of her contemporaries, and always treated them with respect. Jamie Hammerstein recalled a transcontinental train trip his family and Dorothy took together, and how Dorothy would pointedly spend time with him, then a small boy, in the observation car.)

Kern also admired Dorothy for her good taste, in clothes and everything else—something Kern cared about and felt deeply. He also taught her about antiques, and she would accompany him to auctions. For their daily treks to the studio, Dorothy would swing by and pick him up, because he didn't drive. At one point (which she liked to cite later in life as the only time Kern was really difficult with her) she bought a Cord automobile. George Gershwin had begun teaching her to play golf down in Palm Springs, and as they made the trip in his new Cord, she fell in love with it. He said,

"Well, why don't you get one, too?" and with his encouragement she did, and had it painted bright blue, the color of the pencils she liked to use. The day after it was delivered, she proudly arrived to pick up Kern for his lift to the studio, but instead of the admiration and congratulations she expected, he lit into her about the car's vulgarity, complaining that he didn't want to be seen driving in anything so coarse a color. He gave her such a hard time about it that she acquiesced and took it back to be painted black. Even then, he kept badgering her to get rid of it, saying that the Cord company was going to go out of business. She did, and it did.

Lily Pons had made her screen debut the year before *I Dream Too Much* was released, in *One Night of Love*, which also featured fellow Met opera divas Grace Moore and Gladys Swarthout. *Dream* would be Pons's chance to shine, without the others around. Pons was a tiny French coloratura as famous for not being able to go onstage to sing until she'd thrown up as she was for her trills. She charmed millions. She wore tiny couture clothes and spoke very fast in a very high, tiny, French-accented voice—and was virtually impossible to understand.

It was not Dorothy's first brush with her. Several years earlier Pons had summoned the team of Fields and McHugh, in a much publicized move, to help her prepare for a national concert tour by providing her with some contemporary American material. In New York's swank Essex House hotel across from Central Park they met, and while the press took pictures of the three of them at the piano, the opera star elaborated on her plans to put herself more in touch with the American people. "American songs have a certain distinction of style that makes them different," she announced. Dorothy and McHugh had already begun planning the kinds of things that would suit her, and for an upcoming radio broadcast wrote her a song called "Will You Remember, Will You Forget."

I Dream Too Much didn't require Pons to play against type. When RKO sent out their thumbnail sketch for publicity purposes, they described it as "the story of an amazing little French girl who runs away from fame and into the arms of love, is overtaken by it

IF 1935 WAS "OFFICIALLY" THE YEAR THAT JAZZ BECAME "SWING,"

Dorothy's new association with Jerome Kern seemed to be leading her in the opposite direction. Fields's naturally swingy lyrics had met Kern's operetta-scented music, and their first full assignment together following *Roberta* was *I Dream Too Much*. Another of Dorothy's "opera singer projects" (like the one for Tibbett), this time the mark was Met coloratura Lily Pons (next in line would be Grace Moore). Petite, French, couture-clad, Pons had known Dorothy some years earlier, when the singer had approached Fields and McHugh to supply her with some concert material that would enhance her image with the American public as "one of the folks." The score for *I Dream Too Much*, however, particularly its title song, was firmly on Pons's turf. But Dorothy wasn't the only one of her crowd who was seeming to go operatic; the same year, George Gershwin unveiled *Porgy and Bess*.

Dorothy Fields, Jimmy McHugh, Metropolitan opera tenor Tito Schipa, and coloratura Lily Pons when the singer called on the star songwriters to aid her image by supplying her with something to sing besides the Bell Song from *Lakme*.

I DREAM TOO MUCH

I dream too much, but if I dream
too much
I only dream to touch your heart
again.
I close my eyes to see
Your hand, your smile, your joy
in loving me.

We dance and sing, we steal a
touch of spring,

I dream of everything we two
have known,
And yet my dreams have shown
Perhaps I dream too much
alone.

Um-m-m-m
Perhaps I dream too much
alone.

and tries desperately to escape from its manacles so she can just live and love a rose-hued life of romance."

(You could also say that Pons plays a singing student who runs away from her lessons and a tyrannical uncle to a carnival, where she meets Henry Fonda, an overlooked American composer, and marries him after a night of drinking. When Pons goes to a great impresario to convince him of the merits of Fonda's music, she is, instead, discovered and becomes a big star, while Fonda becomes a cab driver. They meet again years later, and when he refuses her offer to give up everything for him, she produces his opera as an operetta in London, where it becomes a big hit, so, true to '30s Hollywood, he feels able to be reunited with her after all.)

Pons showcased her operatic talents with the "Bell Song" from *Lakme* and "Caro Nome" from *Rigoletto*, and a lot of people dubbed the movie *I Scream Too Much*. She also showcased, courtesy of her *Lakme* costume, her bare navel, which upset censor Joseph Breen no end, and in the to-do that followed, he solemnly wrote the studio claiming that he'd actually heard audiences "tittering" at the sight.

Also featured in the cast were character actors Eric Blore (who always played parts like the manservant in Astaire-Rogers movies) and the manic Mischa Auer, plus a beginner named Lucille Ball, who'd appeared as one of the models in *Roberta*. Astaire alter ego Hermes Pan choreographed the dances. At the Radio City Music Hall premiere in 1935, the show included the Music Hall Symphony Orchestra playing a "Medley of Jerome Kern Melodies."

Kern and Fields had written four songs for *I Dream Too Much*: "Jockey on the Carrousel," "I'm the Echo," "I Got Love," and "I Dream Too Much." The forcing together of different styles into one story didn't go unnoticed by the press, which found the songs and dances pleasant, but out of place. Nevertheless, the title song went on to become a big popular success of the year. Compared to a lot of the other Kern-Fields collaborations, and perhaps because of the "operatic" parameters, time hasn't been too kind to the score. Only the flowery title song survives as a standard—but barely.

After *I Dream Too Much*, Dorothy and Kern were firmly established as a team. Their next project was the new Fred Astaire and Ginger Rogers picture, for which Pandro Berman had signed Kern, and Kern had again requested Dorothy. Its working title was *I Won't Dance* (the song title that seemed destined to bounce from one project to another).

The Astaire-Rogers movies of the 1930s are perhaps the single most concentrated cinematic repository for bedrock chunks of the American songbook. An assignment that was almost a badge of honor for songwriters, each one was engineered by a mainstay of popular music: *Top Hat* and *Follow the Fleet* by Irving Berlin; *Shall We Dance* by George and Ira Gershwin; *Flying Down to Rio* by Vincent Youmans (with lyricists Edward Eliscu and Gus Kahn); and *Roberta* and *Swing Time* (which was what *I Won't Dance* finally became) by Jerome Kern and Dorothy Fields. More than most other movie musical scores of the period, each one packs in hit after standard. *The Gay Divorcée* (1934) included Cole Porter's "Night and Day" and Herb Magidson and Con Conrad's huge hit "The Continental." *Top Hat* (1935) had "Cheek to Cheek," "Isn't This a Lovely Day," "No Strings," and "Top Hat, White Tie and Tails." *Follow the Fleet* (1936) had "Let Yourself Go," "I'm Putting All My Eggs in One Basket," "Let's Face the Music and Dance," and "We Saw the Sea." *Shall We Dance* (1937) had "Beginner's Luck," "Let's Call the Whole Thing Off," "Shall We Dance?," "Slap That Bass," "They All Laughed," and "They Can't Take That Away from Me." Even the antique *Flying Down to Rio* (1933), the first teaming of Astaire and Rogers, which featured them in smaller roles, contained "Carioca," "Flying Down to Rio," and "Music Makes Me." *Swing Time* (1936) would prove no different.

Pandro S. Berman, the architect of it all, had faced the task of developing the musical film only a few years after the arrival of sound, and he made pioneering strides in creating a semblance of naturalism and sanity in the bizarre, otherworldly mind-set and production techniques of early movie musicals. Dorothy later recalled the awkwardness of her first movie efforts: "In those days there was the theory that every time you did a song in a picture, it had to be

THE LYRICIST FRED EBB, WHO WITH COMPOSER

John Kander is known for writing such shows as *Flora, the Red Menace, Cabaret, Zorba*, and *Chicago*, considered Dorothy his mentor. Ebb, who came to prominence in the 1960s, first met Dorothy early in his career. "Dorothy and Herb were about to write the libretto for a musical based on Eugene O'Neill's *Ah, Wilderness*," he recalls. "The people that represented me at the time thought I ought to write four or five songs 'on spec' in order to audition for Herbert and Dorothy and possibly get the job (it would have been my first) of writing the score for that show.

"We did write five songs and we auditioned for the two of them one spring day. I was unbearably nervous, but all thorough the audition, I can still recall Miss Fields smiling at me and encouraging me, and nodding her head, 'yes.' When we had finished, nobody said anything (I think they were asked not to), and Dorothy walked me to the door of the office in which we had played. As I was going out, she impulsively kissed me on the cheek and said, 'I wish I were in your shoes right now.' I took it to mean that she envied my youth and (as she later told me) was really impressed with my talent. I still do, and always will remember that afternoon. The show, of course, never happened. Herb and Dorothy had a dispute with David Merrick, who was the producer, and so I was never considered for the show again. But I always will remember her for her kindness and how whenever she saw me for years after that, she always stopped, hugged me, and asked how I was doing."

"Pick Yourself Up" was the only song besides "A Fine Romance" for which Dorothy wrote the lyrics first and had Kern follow her lead, the implications of which are interesting if you consider that the song's catchy rhythms are actually driven by the words. After singing the song for decades, Rosemary Clooney finally recorded "Pick Yourself Up" for an album about mothers and daughters.

"Musically as well as lyrically, there's something important going on there," she says. "It's such a perfect marriage of music and words. I used to sing it a lot. Nelson Riddle did an arrangement for my television show in the '50s. I know it sounds like a cliché, but there really is something about it that makes you feel better. In the song, she hits all the reasons for you to do it. If there is a song that I can play whenever I'm on that downside, that's the one. With the album, I'd be playing it through before a concert or something while I make up—and I'll always make sure that 'Pick Yourself Up' is the very last thing I hear before I go onstage."

PICK YOURSELF UP

Please teacher, teach me some-
    thing,
Nice teacher, teach me some-
    thing
I'm as awkward as a camel,
That's not the worst,
My two feet haven't met yet,
But I'll be teacher's pet yet,
'Cause I'm gonna learn to dance
    or burst.

Nothing's impossible I have
    found,
For when my chin is on the
    ground,
I pick myself up, dust myself off,
Start all over again.

Don't lose your confidence if you
    slip,
Be grateful for a pleasant trip,
And pick yourself up, dust your-
    self off,
Start all over again.

Work like a soul inspired,
'Til the battle of the day is won.
You may be sick and tired,
But you'll be a man, my son!

Will you remember the famous
    men,
Who had to fall to rise again?
So take a deep breath,
Pick yourself up,
Dust yourself off,
Start all over again.

excused by having a guitar or a banjo on
the set. They felt that you could not,
shall we say, 'square' music in a picture
unless you could see an instrument
playing the music." For example, in
Love in the Rough, the Robert
Montgomery film she'd worked on
in 1930, "the caddies had little har-
monicas. Every time we did a
song, the caddies would accompany this love song—behind the
bushes—and then the music could
creep in."

The most common premise for a character busting out with a
song, of course, was the "show within a show" device. While
Berman's Astaire-Rogers films certainly availed themselves of this
convenience for certain numbers, Berman made the musicals more
cinematic by freeing the stories up from the *necessity* of using it.
Sure, Fred Astaire was still always the American dancer who one
way or another winds up performing with the hotel's band. On the
other hand, he also sang "Isn't This a Lovely Day (to Be Caught in
the Rain)" to Ginger Rogers in a gazebo in the park in the rain—
just because he had something to say to her.

Berman wasn't always met with encouragement. When he
bought *The Gay Divorce* for an Astaire-Rogers vehicle after seeing
it in New York, producer Lou Brock, who'd produced *Flying Down
to Rio* the year before, unceremoniously told him he could "blow a
better script out of his nose."

Nevertheless, nobody could argue with the box office success
of the Astaire-Rogers pictures, which were put out at the approxi-
mate rate of one or two a year. By the time *Swing Time* (or *Never
Gonna Dance*, as it was now called) went into production, the formula was already set. Directed by George Stevens (with playwright
Howard Lindsay coauthor of the screenplay), Fred plays an
American dancer who's engaged to an heiress (played by future con-
sumer journalist Betty Furness), which complicates his getting
together as a team with dancer/dance instructor Ginger. The cast
also included Victor Moore and Helen Broderick.

Dorothy and Kern wrote *Swing Time* in the first few months of
1936. This time, the work proved to be a little different than before.

First, Astaire wanted two thoroughly contemporary dance numbers, which made Kern uneasy, because jazz wasn't in his vocabulary. His melodic lines were long and lyrical, in the traditional vein. For all his genius, a swinging guy he was not—and the idea of jazzing things up always made Kern uncomfortable. To write "Bojangles of Harlem," a tribute to Bill Robinson, they congregated at Dorothy's house, joined by Astaire, who spent a couple of afternoons dancing all around the various rooms and up and down the staircase so Kern could get the feel of the syncopated rhythms as he sat at the piano.

Dorothy also broke with her custom by writing two of the lyrics before the melodies—the only time, she said, she ever did. The first lyric was for "Pick Yourself Up" (whose word rhythms may have contributed to the syncopation, as Astaire's feet had done with "Bojangles"). The other came when Kern told her that they needed "a sarcastic love ballad." She went home and wrote the lyric to "A Fine Romance" and presented it to him completed. Also in the score were the slightly bluesy, rhythmic "Never Gonna Dance" and "Waltz in Swing Time," the other dance number Astaire had required, which Kern put together with orchestrator Robert Russell Bennett.

The song that would be the score's most enduring ballad, however, and would win them both an Academy Award that year was "The Way You Look Tonight"—a lyrical, quintessentially Jerome Kern melody, with its fluid momentum and feel not unlike "Smoke Gets in Your Eyes."

Kern had been the one to suggest the change of the picture's title to *Swing Time*; that, and the fact that today the score represents the cream of Kern's Hollywood work, makes it especially ironic that when the picture opened, a lot of the press considered it a disappointment, carping that Kern had thrown over his traditional "Kernness" to try and swing. One critic even wrote, "Right now we could not even whistle a bar of 'A Fine Romance,' and that's about the catchiest and brightest in the show."

While Kern's music didn't have the immediacy of the Irving Berlin Astaire-Rogers scores, the public, the ages, and the Motion Picture Academy didn't agree with the faultfinders, and every song in *Swing Time* went on to become a classic. That year, 1936, five out

SHELDON HARNICK, THE LYRICIST RESPONSIBLE

(with composer Jerry Bock) for the shows *Fiorello!, She Loves Me*, and *Fiddler on the Roof*, among others, belonged to the generation of songwriters that matured in the late 1950s and 1960s, furthering the musical theatre tradition at a time when America's popular music, engineered by Dorothy and her contemporaries, was supplanted by rock and roll.

Says Harnick, "For me, one of Dorothy Fields's special gifts was her magical ability to mix sophisticated and imaginative ideas with utterly prosaic, 'kitchen sink' words and images, resulting in lyrics of a remarkably appealing freshness. This was a balancing act requiring an impeccable ear and an unusual sense of selectivity—and she had them both.

"A splendid example is 'A Fine Romance.' How I envy the mind which could come up with: 'We should be like a couple of hot tomatoes/But you're as cold as yesterday's mashed potatoes.' And this memorably unhackneyed couplet is followed a moment later by the equally wry lines: 'I've never mussed the crease in your blue serge pants / I never get the chance / This is a fine romance.'

"Rather than quoting the entire lyric, let me simply pay the ultimate tribute one lyricist can pay another and acknowledge that 'A Fine Romance' is one of the many Dorothy Fields lyrics I wish I had written!"

A FINE ROMANCE

A fine romance! With no kisses!
A fine romance, my friend, this is!
We should be like a couple of hot tomatoes,
But you're as cold as yesterday's mashed potatoes.

A fine romance! You won't nestle,
A fine romance! You won't wrestle!
I might as well play bridge with my old maid aunts!
I haven't got a chance.
This is a fine romance.

A fine romance! My good fellow!
You take romance! I'll take Jello!
You're calmer than the seals in the Arctic ocean,
At least they flap their fins to express emotion;

A fine romance! With no quarrels!
With no insults, and all morals!
I've never mussed the crease in your blue serge pants,
I never get the chance
This is a fine romance.

A fine romance! With no kisses!
A fine romance, my friend, this is!
We two should be like clams in a dish of chowder;
But we just "fizz" like parts of a Seidlitz powder.

A fine romance, with no clinches,
A fine romance, with no pinches,
You're just as hard to land as the "Ile de France"
I haven't got a chance,
This is a fine romance!

A fine romance! My dear Duchess!
Two old fogies who need crutches!
True love should have the thrills that a healthy crime has!
We don't have half the thrills that the "March of Time" has!

A fine romance, my good woman!
My strong "aged-in-the-wood" woman!
You never give the orchids I send a glance!
No! You like cactus plants,
This is a fine romance!

of the six songs were hits, topped by "The Way You Look Tonight," which was number two on the Hit Parade, and "Bojangles of Harlem"; the others were "A Fine Romance," "Pick Yourself Up," and "Waltz in Swing Time." Only "Never Gonna Dance" was not. Perhaps the most complex and least accessible of the group, the sensual, haunting amalgam of melody and lyric is one of the team's greatest, as time has shown. It also provided one of the loveliest moments in any of the Astaire-Rogers movies, asserting as it does that if he can't dance with her, there can be nobody else, and he'll never dance again.

Just as the score marked a change for Kern's music, so it represented a new plateau for Dorothy's style and expertise. The direct clarity and appeal of the music (as opposed to the opera-flavored *I Dream Too Much*) brought out the things she did best. The *Swing Time* lyrics reject starry-eyed romanticism for smart, urbane, sarcasm-tinged expressions. "Perhaps I dream too much alone" becomes "I might as well play bridge with my old maid aunts."

Dorothy could return to the slangy, edgy voice that had made the McHugh songs like "I Can't Give You Anything but Love" and "On the Sunny Side of the Street" exceptional. But layered on now to the verbal facility and plainspoken imagery was an emotional deepening and sophistication. True, "Pick Yourself Up" is a bouncy, optimistic sentiment along the lines of "Sunny Side," but it also has an underlying wisdom to it—advice given by an older sister or to a son or daughter, rather than a morale-boosting Depression anthem. "A Fine Romance" makes its point:

> We two should be a couple of hot tomatoes,
> But you're as cold as yesterday's mashed potatoes.

The song's conceit is a lyricist's dream, each successive image and rhyme topping the one before. But it's downright rueful, as is, in a completely different way, "Never Gonna Dance," with its quintessentially Fieldsian summing up in slangy erudition, "*la belle, la* perfectly swell romance."

"The Way You Look Tonight" is as romantic a ballad as they come, but unlike Otto Harbach's lyric for "Smoke Gets in Your Eyes," for instance, which is filled with elevated language like "So I chaffed them, and I gaily laughed," the Fields lyric for "The Way You Look Tonight" is restrained, contemplative and matter-of-factly, with wisdom, looking into the future. The phrasing and rhyming, too, show an elegant restraint:

> Lovely,
> Never, never change
> Keep that breathless charm
> Won't you please arrange it
> 'Cause I love you
> Just the way you look tonight

The songs Dorothy wrote with Kern for *Swing Time* are a culmination of their work together. Sexy, sophisticated, shimmering,

The days in Hollywood that Dorothy would remember as "a golden time." Dorothy flanked by partner Jerome Kern and pal George Gershwin

MICHAEL FEINSTEIN, WHO ORIGINALLY ENTERED

the world of American songwriting as Ira Gershwin's assistant, had been introduced to Gershwin by June Levant, the widow of composer Oscar, who collaborated with Dorothy on the score of the 1935 Ginger Rogers vehicle *In Person*.

"Oscar Levant said about Dorothy that she was always writing songs with negative words in the titles," Feinstein says, "like 'I Can't Give You Anything But Love' and one of my favorite songs, which she wrote with Levant called 'Don't Mention Love to Me,' and 'Never Gonna Dance.' It's interesting, because Ira Gershwin said that George was always saying, 'Don't put negative words in the title, because it won't be successful.' But of course two of Ira's biggest hits were 'But Not For Me,' and 'I Can't Get Started.'

"'Never Gonna Dance' is a dark song, and I think that was at a time, during the Depression, when people related to what Fields was saying. It's not an uplifting song. It's a great song; but there's something about it that always leaves a bittersweet feeling. It's poignant. It's sort of a metaphor for all of our lives: 'I'm not going to do what I love best, because it's not going to bring the fulfillment.'

"Dorothy Fields must have been keenly aware that she was a successful woman in a man's world. And I think she was successful by not compromising herself. Dorothy Fields was a woman with balls. She is so saucy and spicy. I can't think of another woman writer of that time who expressed what she expressed not only with the wit and eloquence, but with the courage and the nerve."

Mutual admiration society.
Jerome Kern and Dorothy Fields
at work in Hollywood, 1936

NEVER GONNA DANCE

Though I'm left without a penny,
The wolf was discreet; he left me
 my feet,
And so, I put them down on anything
But the La Belle, La perfectly
 swell romance,
Never gonna dance, never
 gonna dance,
Only gonna love, never gonna
 dance.

Have I a heart that acts like a
 heart,
Or is it a crazy drum,
Beating the weird tattoos
Of the St. Louis blues?

Have I two eyes to see your two
 eyes;
Or see myself on my toes,
Dancing to radios
For Major Edward Bowes.

I'll put my shoes on beautiful
 trees,

I'll give my rhythm back to the
 breeze,
My dinner clothes may dine
 where they please,
For all I really want is you;

And to Groucho Marx I give my
 cravat,
To Harpo goes my shiny silk hat,
To heaven I give a vow to adore
 you;
I'm starting now to be much
 more positive that

Though I'm left without a penny,
The wolf was not smart; he
 left me my heart
And so I'll never go for anything
But the La Belle, La perfectly
 swell romance,
Never gonna dance, never
 gonna dance,
Only gonna love you,
Never gonna dance.

"THE WAY YOU LOOK TONIGHT" WON DOROTHY

an Academy Award at age thirty, and remains one of the American songbook's finest entries. Singer Mary Cleere Haran has devoted considerable energy to the work of Dorothy Fields, including a Fields and Kern show at New York's Rainbow and Stars and a portion of her *Live at the Algonquin* album.

"They used to say about Fred and Ginger that he gave her class and she gave him sex," she says. "For me, the Kern-Fields collaboration is the same. It was Kern's gorgeous and sumptuous melodies that freed Dorothy to express a lot more than she had with McHugh. The Kern-Fields songs have real depth, especially their ballads. Dorothy often told this story about 'The Way You Look Tonight': 'The first time Jerry played that melody for me I had to leave the room because I started to cry. The release absolutely killed me. I couldn't stop, it was so beautiful.'

"For me, the lyric is equally beautiful:

> Someday, when I'm awfully low,
> When the world is cold,
> I will feel a glow just thinking of you
> And the way you look tonight.

"A complete sentence, masterfully written, expressing a full thought. Its irony is contained in the fact that the speaker is predicting that this moment will be one of the most beautiful in her life and the object of her love is frozen in a planned instance of nostalgia knowing that this will never be again, loving her object in both the present and future. I think this is the most beautiful song ever written."

Fred and Ginger, *Swing Time*

THE WAY YOU LOOK TONIGHT

Someday, when I'm awfully low,
When the world is cold,
I will feel a glow just thinking of
   you
And the way you look tonight.

Oh, but you're lovely,
With your smile so warm,
And your cheek so soft,
There is nothing for me but to
   love you,
Just the way you look tonight.

With each word your tenderness
   grows,
Tearing my fear apart,
And that laugh that wrinkles your
   nose
Touches my foolish heart.

Lovely, never, never change,
Keep that breathless charm,
Won't you please arrange it,
'Cause I love you,
Just the way you look tonight,
Just the way you look tonight.

Thirty-year-old Oscar winner. Dorothy on Academy Awards night, after receiving her honor for "The Way You Look Tonight"

there is a magic to them that seems to preserve the peak golden days of life in Hollywood.

When the Motion Picture Academy presented Dorothy with her Oscar for "The Way You Look Tonight," it was the first time in its history it had honored a female songwriter. Thirty-year-old Dorothy, needless to say, was ecstatic. Her father, who'd tried so hard to keep her out of show business, didn't even attempt to contain his pride. Lew wrote to her a few months later, "Your lyrics are great, funny stuff. I'm just coo-coo about them. . . ."

Dorothy, in fact, had already written another hit song in 1936, without Kern, when she took an assignment on loan to Paramount. It was for yet another opera star vehicle, a picture called *The King Steps Out*, featuring Grace Moore and Franchot Tone, and the studio asked Dorothy to put a lyric to a Fritz Kreisler melody from his old operetta *Apple Blossom*. Dorothy had never met Kreisler, but she took the song home and came back with "Stars in My Eyes" (along the lines of "I Dream Too Much"), which immediately become enormously popular and a top song of the year. Dorothy liked to recall later that she eventually received a note from Kreisler that said,

"Thank you, Miss Fields." "Not what you'd call high praise," she'd comment. But then she recalled that after Oscar Hammerstein worked for three weeks on the lyric for "Lover Come Back to Me," for *New Moon*, Sigmund Romberg's only remark was "It fits."

After the ceremony and laurels surrounding her Academy Award, Dorothy resumed her life and work. She was enjoying both as much as ever: the daily sessions with Kern; the incessant parties and goings on at her own home, or nightspots like the Mocambo, or at friends' houses, like the Beverly Hills digs (belonging to Lawrence Tibbett) rented jointly by songwriting team Harold Arlen and Yip Harburg; the daily games of tennis at George and Ira Gershwin's poolside court.

"It was a very pleasant life. The musical people gravitated toward each other. We had wonderful parties at the Hammersteins, and George and Ira's. We used to play around all the time out there. It was a wonderful, rosy period."

Dorothy would later recall that more often than not, on the way home after a party, Kern (and Romberg as well) would be hurt and irate that George Gershwin was always asked to play and had just spent the evening monopolizing the piano, while hordes of admirers hung on his every note. The truth was that Kern's way around a piano, while fine for his composing, couldn't approach Gershwin's virtuosity, but Dorothy could never bring herself to tell him that.

Swing Time would be the pinnacle of Dorothy's work with Kern, and would mark the height of her Hollywood experience. Though she continued to work and live there for a time, things would soon begin to change.

Dorothy's next project with Kern was again for Grace Moore, this time a picture with Cary Grant first called *Interlude*, then finally *When You're in Love*, about an opera singer marrying for U.S. citizenship. The team provided a couple of songs, not particularly notable compared with the work they had been exhibiting lately. The following year they wrote the score for a screwball comedy with Irene Dunne and Douglas Fairbanks, Jr., called *The Joy of Living*.

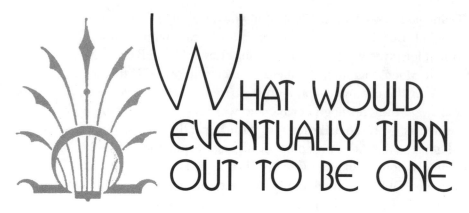

WHAT WOULD EVENTUALLY TURN OUT TO BE ONE

of Jerome Kern's catchiest tunes, "You Couldn't Be Cuter," began life in a bizarrely square rendition by Kern's schoolboy crush, Irene Dunne, in 1938's *The Joy of Living*. After Kern had loosened up his propensity for swinging with his score for *Swing Time* two years earlier, Dunne introduced the song, her lyric soprano diligently on the beat, as a lullaby to twin child actresses, while accompanying herself on a white toy piano.

Irene Dunne introducing the Kern-Fields standard "You Couldn't Be Cuter" in *The Joy of Living*, 1938

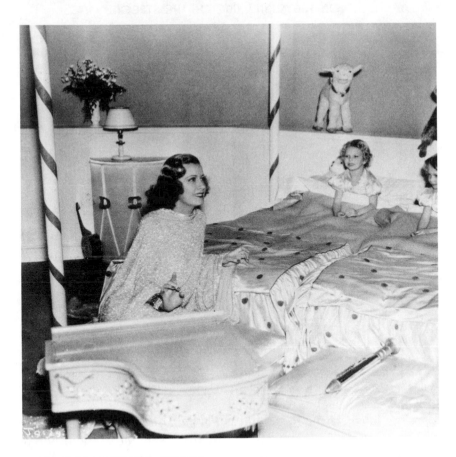

YOU COULDN'T BE CUTER

Your poise! Your pose!
That cute fantastic nose!
You're mighty like a knockout,
You're mighty like a rose!

I'm sold, I'm hooked!
The well-known goose is
 cooked!
You got me little fella,
I'm sunk! I'm gone! I'm hooked!

You couldn't be cuter
Plus that you couldn't be smarter
Plus that intelligent face
You have a disgraceful charm
 for me.

You couldn't be keener,
You look so fresh from the
 cleaner,

You are the little grand slam
I'll bring to my family,

My ma will show you an album
 of me
That'll bore you to tears!
And you'll attract all the
 relatives we
Have dodged for years and
 years

And what'll they tell me?
Exactly what'll they tell me?
They'll say you couldn't be nicer,
Couldn't be sweeter,
Couldn't be better
Couldn't be smoother,
Couldn't be cuter,
Baby, than you are.

Another opera singer project: Met star Grace Moore and Franchot Tone in *The King Steps Out*, 1936, Dorothy's absentee collaboration with Fritz Kreisler

The Joy of Living began life as *The Joy of Loving*, until the censors began to think about what exactly that might mean and ordered it changed. Kern was absolutely mad for Irene Dunne, personally and professionally, and worked with her whenever possible. After *Roberta*, she was cast as Magnolia in the film version of *Show Boat* (opposite Allan Jones). In *The Joy of Living*, she played a Broadway actress hounded by playboy Fairbanks, who tries to get her to chuck all the hard work and run away to a desert island with him. (Again, Lucille Ball shows up in the cast, this time as Dunne's annoying younger sister.)

The original story had been devised by Dorothy with her brother Herb, but in Hollywood style of the time, the studio brought in other writers to write the screenplay. It wasn't really a musical at all, but a comedy with songs, and it would turn out to be Irene Dunne's last big singing movie. The group of songs that Dorothy and Kern provided, including "Just Let Me Look at You," "Heavenly Party" and "What's Good About Goodnight?," also yielded one of their great standards, "You Couldn't Be Cuter."

But before they could finish work on them, two things happened that would cast a pall over Dorothy's remaining time in

Hollywood. First, Kern suffered a heart attack followed by a stroke, and lay gravely ill and then bedridden for some four months. He was too ill, in fact, to be told of the second event, which shocked and horrified the entire world, but particularly the small community of friends and colleagues. That was the news that George Gershwin had died of a brain tumor, at age 39.

Dorothy, along with everybody else, was devastated by Gershwin's death. She and the rest of the Fields family felt the loss especially acutely. Nobody could fathom how it could be true, how Gershwin, who'd always exuded health, virility, and good-time humor, could be cut down like that. He and Dorothy were close social pals. The Fieldses' hearts went out to the Gershwin family, particularly Ira, who would never really recover for the rest of his life.

Hardest hit of all the Fields clan was Herb, who not only had been close to the brothers but had been their collaborator on the failed Broadway show *Pardon My English* several years earlier. Herb lapsed into a deep depression, which only exacerbated the discouragement he had been experiencing on and off since he'd had his last successes. (He would, however, come back with another huge Broadway hit the following year, collaborating, as he'd done so

Ginger Rogers as a glamorous movie star fleeing to the country in 1935's *In Person*, with George Brent

IF YOU HAD TO SINGLE OUT ONE SONG

as the finest example of a Dorothy Fields lyric, the overwhelming temptation is "Remind Me." There are other candidates, particularly "The Way You Look Tonight," or as a theatre song, "He Had Refinement." But as a popular song lyric, "Remind Me" is not only perfect, it couldn't have been written by anybody else. From the first line—the colloquial admonition, "Turn off that charm"—it is quintessentially Fieldsian.

Cannibalized from an earlier score with Kern and used in the 1940 Abbott and Costello movie *One Night in the Tropics,* "Remind Me" was first sung by Allan Jones. But it is distinctly a woman's song, and probably the best argument for the case that Dorothy Fields's popular song lyrics are essentially feminine in viewpoint (a case impossible to prove, with opinions firmly on both sides). While clearly Dorothy's work has the weight and edge of any of her male contemporaries, there is undeniably a feminine brain at work. The first few lines of "Remind Me"'s verse is the anatomy of an "on the other hand" woman's mental process. Irving Berlin might have put himself in a woman's place to write "I Got Lost in His Arms," but only a woman could have written that verse to "Remind Me" (her work has been called "hormonal"). The conceit of the song follows suit (it also has the triple end rhymes Dorothy liked to use, like "met you/let you/forget you"), and the brilliance of the lyric culminates in its last line—the surprising, deft mental turnaround that "buttons up" the end of the song.

Lou Costello, Mexican bombshell Nina Orla in her debut, and Bud Abbott in *One Night in the Tropics*, 1940, which introduced one of Kern and Fields's finest songs, "Remind Me"

REMIND ME

Turn off that charm,
I'm through with love for awhile
I'm through, and yet
You have a fabulous smile,
So if I forget

Remind me
Not to find you so attractive,
Remind me
That the world is full of men,

When I start to miss you,
To touch your hand,
To kiss you,
Remind me
To count to ten!
I had a feeling when I met you
You'd drive me crazy, if I'd
    let you,
But all my efforts to forget you
Remind me I'm in love again.

I get my heart well in hand and
    I'm certain
That I can take you or leave you
    alone,

Then you begin that beguine
    again
And boom! I give in again,
I have a will made of steel my
    friend,
But when it seems about to
    bend,

Remind me
Not to mention that I love you.
Remind me
To be sorry that we met.
Although I adore you
Remind me to ignore you,
You're one thing I will regret.

So when your charm begins to
    blind me,
I'll simply tie my hands behind
    me,
Don't let me kiss you, please
    remind me,
Unless, my darling, you forget.

well a decade earlier, with Cole Porter on *DuBarry Was a Lady*.)

As the 1930s drew to a close, it seemed more and more to Dorothy that the sunny Beverly Hills days of tennis by the pool and easy studio money had lost their appeal. She turned her attention back to Broadway, which, after languishing in the Depression, was showing signs of supporting life again.

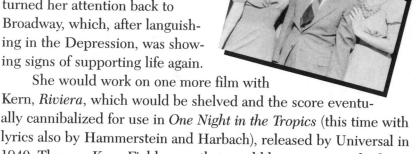

She would work on one more film with Kern, *Riviera*, which would be shelved and the score eventually cannibalized for use in *One Night in the Tropics* (this time with lyrics also by Hammerstein and Harbach), released by Universal in 1940. The one Kern-Fields song that would become a standard is arguably Dorothy Fields's best lyric: "Remind Me."

In 1939, however, Dorothy was already back in New York. Once again, the theatre had become the center of her existence.

WHEN DOROTHY returned to New York in 1938, it was to collaborate with her old friend Arthur Schwartz on a show called *Stars in Your Eyes* (not to be confused with her Grace Moore ditty "Stars in *My* Eyes"). But there were other reasons for Dorothy's return as well: she married for the second time. As in her first marriage, her husband wasn't from the show business world with which she completely surrounded herself. Eli Lahm was a solid businessman (he manufactured blouses), whose brother had founded and owned the Lamston's chain of five-and-ten-cent stores. Eli and Dorothy traveled in some of the same circles and had met through friends. Like Jack, Eli was older than Dorothy by some twelve years. They conducted a bicoastal courtship until Dorothy decided it was time to settle down back in New York.

Mr. and Mrs. Lahm set up housekeeping in a large apartment on 57th Street, across from Carnegie Hall, and commenced an orderly life with enough servants to alleviate any day-to-day stresses of running a household. Her first union had been an instantly acknowledged mistake and never developed into any kind of married state; this time Dorothy was ready for the chance to forge a domestic life of her own. She'd always loved children, as shown by the regard with which she treated those belonging to her friends. Within the next few years, as she approached forty, she would give birth to two of her own: David in 1940 and Eliza in 1944.

The year of her return to the Broadway stage, 1939, marked the return of a few others—writers, composers and performers alike—defecting or visiting from Hollywood. Included was a recuperated Jerome Kern, who, partnered once again with Oscar Hammerstein, would produce *Very Warm for May*—a "college" show with an unfortunately brief run, but which yielded their peerless "All the Things You Are."

Eli and Dorothy (right) dressed for a costume party as Weber and Fields. (Inset) Dorothy in the mid-1940s with her children, David and Eliza.

In fact, after a full decade of the Depression, the musical theatre was, with the rest of the country's economy, beginning to pick
up. And it was a very different musical theatre from the one in
which Dorothy had served her apprenticeship. Just as Hollywood
was where everything was happening in the '30s, Broadway would
be the "happening" place in the '40s. *Stars in Your Eyes*—or *Swing
to the Left*, as it was originally called—had a book by J. P. McEvoy,
and was to be a satire drawing on everyone's recent experiences in
Hollywood, a "what would happen if . . ." notion surrounding a leftwing writer (an Orson Welles genius type) getting involved with the
making of a Hollywood plantation epic.

Mostly, producer Dwight Deere Wiman wanted to have a show
running to take advantage of the influx of tourists in town for the
World's Fair. It would be only Dorothy's second book musical (the
first was the cumbersome *Hello Daddy!*), and for the show's stars,
no less than Ethel Merman and Jimmy Durante were engaged,
Merman as the obnoxious movie star/top dog of Monotone Studios
and Durante as the labor organizer, with the added talents of
Richard Carlson (as the writer) and ballerina
Tamara Toumanova.

But when Wiman brought in *wunderkind* director Joshua Logan, who'd had
recent successes with shows such as
Rodgers and Hart's *I Married an Angel*
and Kurt Weill and Maxwell Anderson's
Knickerbocker Holiday, everything began
to change. Mostly, Logan found the leftwing politics part of the satire unfunny
and convinced the creative team that it
would never work. Instead, he argued, it
should be about the mixing of sex and the movie business. Thus began a marathon of undoing, redoing, and mammoth
restructuring. Durante's character became the studio "idea" man,
based on MGM's "Hoppy" Hopkins, who used to pull people aside
with "I'll give you two quick ideas—Gable, Tracy, San Francisco!"
The social commentary disappeared, and the show that emerged
became above all a vehicle tailored to the talents of Merman and
Durante.

Logan later described the process of excising the leftwing
political material as "trickier than brain surgery." Dorothy and

Schwartz had their favorite songs, like the witty "My New Kentucky Home" (which had set grass, the moon, and the rest of nature conforming to union hours) and "Just a Little Bit More," a nonunion girl's lament for Merman, and they were able to talk Logan into keeping them. But during the New Haven tryout, not only did the show run an hour overtime, it became apparent that "My New Kentucky Home" among other numbers no longer fit the show at all. Instead, Logan persuaded Dorothy and Schwartz to replace it with a more appropriate number, and they came up with the bawdy, assertive "A Lady Needs a Change." A pure Merman showstopper from the moment it went in, the song remains the most prominently surviving number from *Stars in Your Eyes*.

Other songs included "This Is It" and "I'll Pay the Check," but the height of the evening was "It's All Yours," a duet in which Merman and Durante brought down the house by stopping in the middle of each chorus so Durante could grab a phone from the footlights, or anything else that was handy, and interpolate his own shenanigans right there, with Merman mimicking him (Durante taught her how) and helping him break up the audience. ("Hello, is dis de meat market? Well, meet my wife at six o'clock!") This went on for about ten choruses.

Added treats in the show were Mildred Natwick as a screenwriter, and a chorus that included Alicia Alonzo, Nora Kaye, Maria Karnilova, and Jerome Robbins. Nevertheless, in spite of a fairly favorable critical reception and the great commercial appeal of its two stars, *Stars in Your Eyes* disappointed everyone involved by closing in less than four months. Merman went on, only a few months later, to star in Herb Fields's new venture with Cole Porter, *DuBarry Was a Lady*, which became the biggest hit of the year.

Dorothy was happy to be working back on Broadway. Though she had enjoyed life enormously in California in the last decade and treasured her partnership with Kern, the whole process of movie making was a relatively detached experience for a creative contributor. "In theatre, you're constantly with a show until it opens," she observed later. "You're with it in every phase—the writing, first—and then all through rehearsals, the out of town tryout, until you get to New York. When you write a score for a picture, you write it, and you leave. You don't see it for maybe nine months or a year. You become completely disassociated with it, and you don't even remember what you wrote. That happened to me a couple of times; I was amazed at the songs we had written."

The songs she had written for *Stars in Your Eyes* were immediately of a different color and nature than the body of work she had been turning out in Hollywood, and even from her Broadway revue days of the '20s. "When you're writing for Ethel Merman and Jimmy Durante," she would explain, "you don't write the kind of lyric you'd write for Grace Moore." Though the statement is very true, there is something in her *Stars in Your Eyes* work of a shifting-gears quality, as though she were getting into a different mode.

In fact, she was. It was still a time on Broadway when individual songs in a score were pulled out to become "breakaway" pop hits; the work of Rodgers and Hammerstein hadn't yet introduced the idea of welding everything in a musical together. And yet there was really no break-away song from *Stars in Your Eyes*. That in itself is not so unusual, but Dorothy was a lyricist who, until only a couple of years before, had had five or six top hits a year almost every year going back a decade, with both Kern and McHugh. Arthur Schwartz was no stranger to hits either, as the composer (most often teamed with Howard Dietz) of "Dancing in the Dark," "You and the Night and the Music," and "I Guess I'll Have to Change My Plan," among many other standards.

Obviously, there are many reasons why a particular show may not yield a hit song. In this case one of the reasons was a difference between Dorothy's new songs and the ones she did for Hollywood and the early revues. She began thinking like a dramatist, with considerations such as characterization and developing the narrative as a whole. With *Stars in Your Eyes* she did not fully realize the transformation, but the balance of elements had clearly shifted (she even played with some underscored, rhymed dialogue in the show).

WHEN JEROME AND RHEA CHODOROV WERE FIRST

becoming acquainted with Dorothy, Rhea recalls that Joe's wife, Germaine, took her aside to instruct her. "Germaine admired Dorothy, and I think was a little jealous of her, too, because Dorothy lived like a princess. Germaine said, 'Listen—the next time you're over at their house, get Dorothy to show you her closets.' And the next time I was there, I said to Dorothy, whom I didn't know terribly well, 'I hear you have fabulous closets.' She said, 'Would you like to see them?' I said, 'I'd love it!' So she took me upstairs, and she had different closets for everything. I mean I had one little closet that everything was crammed into. She had closets full of clothes, shoe closets . . . . But the thing that impressed me the most was that she had one large closet just for nightgowns."

Stars in Your Eyes, 1939, the show that brought Dorothy back to New York (in collaboration with Arthur Schwartz) after almost a decade in Hollywood. L to r: Robert Ross, Richard Carlson, Tamara Toumanova, Jimmy Durante, Ethel Merman, Mildred Natwick, and Clinton Sundberg

A LADY NEEDS A CHANGE

It is not within our power
To keep love from getting sour
Ask each one who tries it!
Don't be down or broken
   hearted
When the cooling off gets
   started,
Be big! Recognize it!

When arms are not inviting,
His kiss is not exciting,
When there's no thrill in fighting,
A lady needs a change!

When music doesn't floor you,
The moon does nothing for you,
His face begins to bore you,
A lady needs a change!

Once he looked romantic, so
   romantic
You fell with a crash,
Now he's just a bust, and love
   is just
A warmed up plate of hash.

You yawn at one another.
You treat him like a brother.
He treats you like his mother.
When there's no doubt the
   fire's out
A lady needs a change!

STARS IN YOUR EYES

The entire action of the play takes place on sound stage "7"
of the Monotone Picture Corp., Hollywood, Calif.

ACT I.

1. "Places, Everybody" . . . . .Company

2. "One Brief Moment" . .Walter Cassel, Paul Godkin and Ensemble

3. "This Is It" . . . . .ETHEL MERMAN, Walter Cassel,
   Edward Kane, Robert Shanley, Davis Cunningham

4. "All the Time" .RICHARD CARLSON
   and TAMARA TOUMANOVA

5. "Self Made Man" . . . . .JIMMY DURANTE

6. "Okay for Sound" . . . . .Rennie McEvoy,
   Dawn Roland and Ensemble

7. "A Lady Needs a Change" . . . . .ETHEL MERMAN

8. "Terribly Attractive" . . . . .JIMMY DURANTE
   and MILDRED NATWICK

9. "Just a Little Bit More" . . . . .ETHEL MERMAN

10. "Night Club Ballet" . . . . .TAMARA TOUMANOVA,
    Ted Gary, Dan Daily, Jr., and Ensemble

11. Finale . . . . .ETHEL MERMAN and Ensemble

---

ACT II

1. "As of Today" . . . .Rennie McEvoy, Frances Rands, Mary Wickes,
   Roger Stearns, Kathryn Mayfield, David Morris,
   Betty Hunter, Dan Dailey, Jr., and Ensemble

2. "He's Goin' Home" . . . . .JIMMY DURANTE and Ensemble

3. "I'll Pay the Check" .ETHEL MERMAN

4. "Never a Dull Moment" . . . . .Dawn Roland, Ted Gary,
   Dan Dailey, Jr., Rennie McEvoy,
   Audrey Westphal and Ensemble

5. "This Is It" — Reprise . . . . .ETHEL MERMAN

6. "Court Ballet" . . . . . . .TAMARA TOUMANOVA, Corps de Ballet
   and Walter Cassel, Edward Kane,
   Robert Shanley, Davis Cunningham

7. "It's All Yours" . . . .ETHEL MERMAN and JIMMY DURANTE

8. Finale . . . . .Entire Company

Studio boss Ethel Merman tries her hand at seducing boy genius Carlson in *Stars in Your Eyes*, a Fields-Arthur Schwartz collaboration, directed by Joshua Logan

Throughout the rest of her career she would be diligent about the notion that a musical must be integrated, a lyric part of the greater dramatic entity. She wouldn't always achieve it, but from then on, the challenge would color virtually everything she wrote. And for the most part, her songs would be theatre songs, in the way that Stephen Sondheim's songs are theatre songs—occasionally paying the dividend of a pop hit, but very rarely.

Almost as if to get her bearings, she wrote no lyrics for her next few projects. Instead, she worked on librettos only, collaborating with Herb for three Cole Porter musicals in a row. (Porter wrote both music and lyrics himself, like Irving Berlin.) The shows were *Let's Face It* (1941), *Something for the Boys* (1943), and *Mexican Hayride* (1944). The librettos were pleasant, wacky, slapped together, largely forgettable vehicles for the Porter scores (in these cases, also tuneful but yielding only one of his memorable songs, "I Love You"), and for their stars—designed purely to show audiences a good time. In the days before *Oklahoma!*, for the most part, that's all a book for a musical was supposed to be. Dorothy and Herb would be working, at rehearsals, or in a meeting, and Porter, who didn't really care about the book, would hand them a batch of songs and say, "Here, fit these in." The shows, incidentally, were all big hits that packed in audiences for long runs and made lots of money for everyone involved.

Porter reputedly loved working with any of the Fieldses because when you were out of town and had second-act trouble, he said, they would reach into Lew's trunk and pull out one of his old comic routines or chestnut wheezes to rescue the moment. (Actually, there was a ledger—"the dreaded black ledger"—that used to send the younger Fieldses running in embarrassment in the old Rodgers and Hart show days every time Lew, as producer, suggested dipping in to save whatever dramatic situation needed help. As youngsters, they were all expected to file away "new" material in it. Dorothy and Joe claimed much later, with some glee, that it had been burned up in a fire.)

Cole Porter spirited Danny Kaye away from the company of *Lady in the Dark* to star in *Let's Face It*, which opened in 1941 and did contain one song that would become a Porter standard, "Let's Not Talk About Love." Kaye clowned his way through the story about army wives who adopt three GIs from a nearby base, and audiences kept the show running for 547 performances.

The following year, when work started on *Something for the Boys*, the country was well into World War II. Again, the star was Ethel Merman. It was Merman's fifth Cole Porter show and her fourth consecutive Fields-family show. She had followed *Stars in Your Eyes* and *DuBarry Was a Lady* with Herb and Buddy De Sylva's (and Porter's) next hit, *Panama Hattie*, in 1940 (where it's interesting to note that among the dancing chorus were June Allyson, Betsy Blair, Lucille Bremer, and Vera-Ellen). It was only natural, both on Porter's and the Fieldses' part, to go to Merman with any new project. Also, she happened to be one of Dorothy's closest friends (just as Herb and Porter were close).

Although Porter had completed only three songs and Dorothy and Herb's script was unfinished, Merman immediately agreed. The team's first-choice producer, Vinton Freedley, turned the project down, so Porter promptly called Michael Todd, the flamboyant showman/salesman/gambler who had recently made a splash producing *The Hot Mikado* and, around the time they approached him, *Star and Garter*, a lush Broadway version of Minsky's burlesque, that starred Gypsy Rose Lee and that Louis Kronenberger of *PM* had called "plenty of good, filthy fun." Todd accepted Porter's offer on the spot, without hearing the songs or reading what existed of the script. The team was enough for him.

This time the plot had Merman as a defense worker who inherits a 4,000-acre Texas ranch near the Kelly Field air force base and receives radio messages through a fluke filling in her tooth. Complications ensue. With its good spirits, patriotic theme, and tuneful score, it was a hit with audiences from the beginning. It was also notable for the feud that Merman got into with Paula Laurence, who played one of her competitors for the inheritance (and a

LET'S FACE IT

Music and Lyrics by Cole Porter

Libretto by Dorothy Fields and Herbert Fields

SYNOPSIS OF SCENES

ACT I

Scene 1—The Alicia Allen Milk Farm on Long Island.

Scene 2—The Service Club at Camp Roosevelt, L. I.

Scene 3—A part of the Parade Grounds at Camp Roosevelt.

Scene 4—Mrs. Watson's Summer Home at Southampton, L. I.

ACT II

Scene 1—Mrs. Watson's Home.

Scene 2—The Boathouse of the Hollyhock Inn.

Scene 3—The Hollyhock Inn Gardens.

Scene 4—Exterior of the Inn.

Scene 5—The Service Club at Camp Roosevelt

MUSICAL NUMBERS

ACT I

Milk, Milk, Milk . . . . .Guests at Milk Farm

A Lady Needs a Rest . . . . .Maggie, Nancy and Cornelia

Jerry, My Soldier Boy . . . . .Winnie Potter and Guests

Let's Face It . . . . .Tommy Gleason and The Royal Guards

Ev'rything I Love . . . . .Jerry and Winnie

Ace in the Hole . . . . .Winnie, Muriel, Jean and Ensemble

You Irritate Me So . . . . .Jean and Eddie

Baby Games . . . . .Jerry, Maggie, Frankie, Cornelia, Nancy and Eddie

(a) Fairy Tale . . . . .Jerry

Rub Your Lamp . . . . .Winnie and Ensemble

Specialty Dance:

Cuttin' a Persian Rug . . . . .Mary Parker and Billy Daniel

ACT II

I've Got Some Unfinished Business With You . . . . .Winnie, Jean, Muriel, Dorothy, Gloria, Julian, George and Henry

Let's Not Talk About Love . . . . .Jerry and Maggie

A Little Rumba Numba . . . . .Tommy Gleason, Madge and The Royal Guards

Specialty Dance . . . . .Mary Parker and Billy Daniel

I Hate You, Darling . . . . .Nancy, George, Winnie and Jerry

Melody in Four F . . . . .Jerry

Finale . . . . .Entire Company

The cast of *Let's Face It.* L to r: Eve Arden, Danny Kaye, Edith Meiser, Benny Baker, Jack Williams, and a young Vivian Vance (not shown: an even younger Nanette Fabray)

stripteaser). Merman got upset when, during a comedy number called "By the Mississinewa," Laurence tried to top her laughs by mimicking Merman's own laugh-getting business (it all started with a swing of the braids).

Something for the Boys was also famous for the way Mike Todd handled Merman's absence from the show on several nights with a persistent bout of laryngitis, a potentially disastrous situation. Rather than watch his packed house stampede out on seeing a card in the lobby or a slip in the program announcing that her understudy, Betty Garrett, would go on instead, Todd had leading man Bill Johnson come out in his U.S. Army uniform/costume right before the curtain and read a speech that said Merman was unfortunately ill; after the groans faded, he went on, "There's a little girl who has been waiting in the wings since the show first opened who will appear this evening in the leading role. Tonight that little girl, Betty Garrett, will have her chance. Perhaps you'll see a new star find her place in the Broadway galaxy." Then, before anyone could leave, Todd had the orchestra play "The Star-Spangled Banner," upon which (especially it being wartime) everyone stood at attention. Practically on the final note he rang up the curtain. Anyone heel enough to thwart the man in uniform announcing the Cinderella understudy story, and willing to barrel up the aisle dur-

Brother and sister team. Co-librettists Dorothy and Herbert Fields in the early 1940s

ing the national anthem—well, he was welcome to his refund. Having opened at the Alvin Theatre on January 7, 1943, *Something for the Boys* ran for a year (in 1944 it was made into a movie with Carmen Miranda).

Mexican Hayride, which Todd also produced, did not avail itself of Merman's talents, but those of Bobby Clark, the vaudeville and theatre comedian whose trademark had always been painted-on glasses, and June Havoc, whose childhood as a vaudeville star had been supplanted by adult successes in shows like *Pal Joey*. (She was also Gypsy Rose Lee's sister.) This time, Havoc was playing a lady toreador, with con man Clark hiding out from various authorities in various disguises. Complications, mistaken identities, Havoc tossing Clark a bull's ear, Clark's comic business successively as a tortilla

Ethel Merman and Paula Laurence, "By the Mississinewa"

SOMETHING FOR THE BOYS

Music and lyrics by Cole Porter
Libretto by Dorothy Fields and Herbert Fields

MUSICAL NUMBERS

PROLOGUE

1. "Announcement of Inheritance" . . . . .Calhoun, Chiquita,
Harry and Blossom

ACT I

SCENE 1

2. "See That You're Born in Texas" . . . . .Ensemble

3. "When My Baby Goes to Town" . . . . .Rocky

    Dance by . . . . .Michaela and Ensemble

4. "Something for the Boys" . . . . .Blossom and Boys

5. "When We're Home on the Range" . .Blossom, Chiquita and Harry

SCENE 2

6. "Could It Be You?" . . . . .Rocky and Boys

SCENE 3

7. "Hey, Good Lookin'" . . . . .Blossom and Rocky

8. Reprise: "Hey, Good Lookin'" . . . . .Betty Jean, Corpl. Burns,
and Girls and Boys

SCENE 4

9. "He's a Right Guy" . . . . .Blossom

SCENE 5

10. "Assembly Line" . . . . .Harry, Mary-Frances, Betty-Jean, and Girls

11. "The Leader of a Big Time Band" . . . . .Blossom

    Dance by .Corp. Burns and Ensemble

ACT II.

Musical Numbers

SCENE 1

12. "I'm in Love with a Soldier Boy" . . . . .Mary-Frances,
Girls and Boys

13. "There's a Happy Land in the Sky" . . . . .Blossom, Chiquita,
Harry, Twitch and Rocky

SCENE 3

14. Reprise: "He's a Right Guy" . . . . .Blossom

SCENE 4

15. Waltz Reprise: "Could It Be You?" . . . . .Rocky and Ensemble

16. "By the Mississinewa" . . . . .Blossom and Chiquita

17. "Square Dance" . . . . .The DeMarlos and Ensemble

SCENE 5

18. Dance . . . . .Betty-Jean and Boys

SCENE 6

19. Finale . . . . .Blossom and Entire Company

vendor, in a mariachi band and with fake
teeth, as an Indian maiden (which, critic
Wilella Waldorf in the *Post* observed,
caused him to bear "a haunting resemblance to Katharine Hepburn")—none
of it added up to complete sense.

Like *Something for the Boys*,
Mexican Hayride was directed by
Hassard Short. When it opened for
its Boston tryout the show looked
like it would never come together.
The first rehearsal was such a mess
that it had to be stopped. The costumes were
unwieldy, the numbers and jokes weren't working the way
they were supposed to, and a cellist in the orchestra suffered a fatal
stroke. Things began to turn around when Bobby Clark was allowed
to draw on his signature spectacles. By the time they opened in New
York in late January of 1944, it was a solid hit, and ran even longer
than *Something for the Boys*, closing only after 481 performances.

Immediately on finishing *Hayride*, and after five full years
away from writing lyrics, Dorothy embarked on yet another project
with Todd. The result would be the furthest thing from a Cole
Porter show, but an even bigger hit than any of the last three. And
this time Dorothy would not only coauthor the libretto, but write
the lyrics as well. Todd wanted to do a show with the look and feel
of a Currier and Ives engraving: nineteenth-century nostalgic
Americana. They decided to do something about Central Park and
the "Boss" Tweed scandal. Dorothy and Herb went down to the
New York Times morgue and began going through newspapers of
the period, digging out the particulars of the Tammany Hall graft
and corruption relating to the renovations of Central Park in the
early 1870s. For their story they drew inspiration from the reporting
that exposed and destroyed Tweed and his ring, tipped off by the
inflated prices of park benches, and of sheep to keep the grass down
in Sheep Meadow ($4,000 a sheep).

The result was *Up in Central Park*, and the book centered on a
crusading *Times* reporter out to expose the scandal, who finds love
with the daughter of one of Tweed's cronies. Dorothy and Herb
took it to Sigmund Romberg, who fit Todd's vision of a nineteenth-
century operetta-style treatment.

Mexican Hayride, 1944. June Havoc and comedian Bobby Clark doing the number in which *New York Post* critic Wilella Waldorf described Clark as bearing "a haunting resemblance to Katharine Hepburn"

Sigmund Romberg was a thorough product of the Austro-Hungarian empire, representing the essence of middle European, Viennese-drenched sensibility. He had been writing songs and operettas in the United States since 1914, and championed by the Shuberts, produced a body of work that included *Maytime, Blossom Time, The Student Prince*, and (with Oscar Hammerstein) *The New Moon*, among many others.

Romberg was known as a "card" among the musical and show business crowds. (In a Hollywood biopic based on his life, *Deep in My Heart*, he was portrayed by Jose Ferrer.) He was affectionately recognized for two traits: his bungling of the English language a la Sam Goldwyn, which Hammerstein used to call "Rommyisms," and his cheerful "borrowing" from other composers, which led to Larry Hart's oft-quoted remark to Richard Rodgers, as they listened to Romberg playing Tchaikovsky in the next hotel suite: "Listen, Rommy's doing another score."

Romberg and Dorothy had been friends for years, and when she phoned him to tell him about the new project and he read the script, he was excited. Apart from loving the concept, it had been a long time since he'd had a hit (his last success, not all that successful, had been a full decade earlier). Musically, the world and its swing bands had long since passed him by.

Dorothy wrote some sixteen lyrics to his melodies for the show, which was an amalgam of traditional operetta vocabulary and Broadway show style of the mid-1940s. The songs included "The Fireman's Bride," "When She Walks into a Room," "April Snow," "Carousel in the Park," "The Big Backyard," and a comedy song called "Up from the Gutter," which expressed the soubrette's yen to abandon her Lower East Side Irish background for life among the swells. But the show's premier ballad, destined to become a standard, was "Close as Pages in a Book," in which the lovers affirm their future together.

Rather than mount an expensive production like *Mexican Hayride*, Todd decided to forego elaborate sets and rely on the charm the songs and dances would exert on the audience. There were painted backdrops (designed by Howard Bay) and colorful costumes, and a simulated ice skating ballet (choreographed by Helen Tamiris). Always flamboyant and impetuous, the first day Todd saw the costumes on the cast, he was so displeased that he took a scissors and began cutting them up.

Also, to keep expenses down, there were no stars, but a cast that included Wilbur Evans, Betty Bruce (the dancer who'd also been featured with Merman in *Something for the Boys*), Noah Beery, Sr., and Maureen Cannon.

But when the show tried out in Philadelphia, press and audience response was grim, and Todd got scared. For Broadway, he had booked, to the Shuberts' amazement, the New Century Theatre—a white elephant on the west side of Seventh Avenue, between 58th and 59th streets, well away from even the outskirts of the theatre district—but right next to Central Park. So when it came time for opening night in New York, on January 27, 1945 (a Saturday), Todd pulled out of his sleeve another Mike Todd production. When the show was over, he had lined up practically every horse-drawn carriage in the city and promptly whisked the critics and press, celebri-

MEXICAN HAYRIDE

Music and lyrics by Cole Porter

Libretto by Dorothy Fields and Herbert Fields

SYNOPSIS OF SCENES

ACT I

Scene 1. The Plaza de Toros, Mexico D. F.

Scene 2. The Bedroom De La Reforma Hotel.

Scene 3. The Bar at Ciro's.

Scene 4. A Street in the Merced Market.

Scene 5. An Outdoor Corridor of the National Palace.

Scene 6. Terrace of the Palace at Chepultepec.

ACT II

Scene 1. Xochimilco.

Scene 2. A Gas Station (on the Paseo de la Reforma).

Scene 3. Taxco.

Scene 4. Terrace of the Palace of Chepultepec.

MUSICAL PROGRAM

ACT I

Scene 1.

1. Entrance of Montana . . . . .Principals and Girls and Boys

2. (a) Dance . . . . .Girls and Boys

   (b) Dance . . . . .Marta

Scene 2.

Scene 3.

4. "Sing to Me, Guitar" . . . . .Lolita and Ensemble

   Hermanos Williams Trio

5. "The Good-Will Movement" . . . . .David and Ensemble

   (a) Dance . . . . .Marta Nita, Don Powell and Girls and Boys

   (b) Reprise . . . . .David and Girls

Scene 4.

6. "I Love You" . . . . .David

   (a) Dance . . . . .Paul and Eleanor

   (b) Reprise, "I Love You" . . . . .David

137

ties, and the cast alike through the park (with his influence, probably it was scenically snowing at the time) to Tavern on the Green, where two dance orchestras played and 127 cases of champagne were consumed at a party that went on all night.

Reviews for the show were generally excellent, although the critics had no difficulty seeing through Todd's antics. James Aronson of the *Post* wrote, "It wasn't quite real, last Saturday night . . . I mean riding from the theatre in a brougham (courtesy of Mr. Todd) through the snow-covered hills and meadows of the Park, to a midnight supper for the company (same courtesy) . . . ." The critics also acknowledged Dorothy and Herb's attempt to depart from the everyday Broadway formula. But even if the reviews hadn't been so favorable, with the war drawing to a close, cozy family-style nostalgia was just what the public was in the mood to see. Despite the fact that Herb and Dorothy's book was a bit creaky and stilted (even then), and some critics complained of the show's dullness, *Up in Central Park* was a huge hit, playing to packed houses for almost a year and a half. (Interrupting the subsequent successful road tour,

The skating number, *Up in Central Park*, on Broadway. The 1945 score was Dorothy's first effort as lyricist after a series of libretto-only stints following 1939's *Stars in Your Eyes*

Lifelong friends: Richard Rodgers (a youthful sweetheart) and Oscar Hammerstein II

Todd gambled on staging the show as a spectacular at the Hollywood Bowl, which worked famously for the first week, selling out—until the weather turned foul for the rest of the run.) "Close as Pages in a Book" went on to become a major hit of 1945.

Dorothy, now a mother of two, had a full life as a solid social citizen of wartime New York City. As in all well-to-do urban households of the era, there was a nanny to look after the children, who lived "children's lives"—given their dinner early, and often seeing their mother at odd times in between her work and going out in the evening. Dorothy was one of "the three Dorothys"—the other two being Dorothy Hammerstein, a very close friend, and Dorothy Rodgers, also a good friend. The three, in various combinations, would have lunch together, and, with their husbands, socialize; Dorothy Fields also independently maintained her longtime friendships with Oscar and Dick. Along with her great pal Ethel Merman, among her other close friends were the Berlins, both Irving and his wife, Ellin, who got her involved with charity work on behalf of the Girl Scouts of America.

Along with its success and pleasures, the early '40s also brought the death of Dorothy's father. Lew died in the summer of 1941, around the time she and Herb were in preparations for *Let's*

UP IN CENTRAL PARK

MUSICAL PROGRAM

ACT I.

SCENE ONE

1. "Up From the Gutter" ....Bessie

1a. Reprise "Up From the Gutter" ....Bessie, Rosie,
Danny and Timothy

1b. Dance ....Bessie, Rosie, Danny,
Timothy, Singers and Dancers

2. "Carrousel in the Park" ....Rosie

3. "It Doesn't Cost You Anything to Dream" ....Rosie and John

3a. Reprise "It Doesn't Cost You Anything to Dream" ....Rosie,
Bessie and John

SCENE TWO

4. "Boss Tweed" ....Tweed, Mayor Hall, Connolly,
Sweeney, Monroe, Peters, Timothy and Men

SCENE THREE

5. Opening ....Singing Girls and Boys

6. "When She Walks in the Room" ....John

7. "Currier and Ives" ....Bessie and Joe

7a. Dance ....Bessie, Joe, Daniel and Dancers

8. "Close as Pages in a Book" ....Rosie and John

9. "Rip Van Winkle" ....Rosie, Bessie, Tweed, John,
Joe, Peters and Singers and Dancers

9a. Dance ....Daniel and Dancers

SCENE FOUR

10. Reprise "Close as Pages in a Book" ....John

SCENE FIVE

11. Opening ....Dancers

12. "The Fireman's Bride" ....Rosie, Bessie, Joe,
Daniel and Dancers

13. Reprise "The Fireman's Bride" ....Principals,
Singing Girls and Boys

ACT II

Scene One

14. "When the Party Gives a Party" . . . . Singing Girls and Boys,
Peters, Oakey Hall, Monroe,
Sweeney, Timothy and Danny

15. "Maypole Dance" . . . . .The Dancers

16. "Specialty" . . . . .Joe and Ellen

17. "The Big Back Yard" . . . . .John, Singing Girls and Boys

18. "April Snow" . . . . .Rosie and John

18a. "Finaletto" . . . . .Dancers and Singing Girls and Boys

Scene Four

19. "The Birds and the Bees" .Rosie, Bessie,
Timothy and Danny

Scene Five

20. "Specialty" . . . . .Bessie

Scene Six

21. "The Big Back Yard . . . . .Orchestra

22. Reprise "Close as Pages in a Book" . . . . .Rosie and John

23. Finale . . . . .Entire Company

AFTER HAVING RETURNED TO BROADWAY FROM HOLLYWOOD,

Dorothy spent most of the 1940s as a librettist, until she teamed with Operetta King Sigmund Romberg for *Up in Central Park*, which yielded the hit "Close as Pages in a Book." Unlike George and Ira Gershwin or Rodgers and Hart/Rodgers and Hammerstein, Dorothy had successful collaborations with various people, but never permanent identification as one half of a specific team—which may be a factor in why her name is much less known today than her work. In fact, though her biggest hits were with three main collaborators—McHugh, Kern, and at the end of her life, Cy Coleman—during her career, Dorothy wrote lyrics to the music of eighteen different composers. In chronological order, they were Jimmy McHugh, Reginald Forsythe, Max Steiner, Jerome Kern, Oscar Levant, Fritz Kreisler, Ray Henderson, Arthur Schwartz, Sigmund Romberg, Joseph Meyer, Morton Gould, Harold Arlen, Harry Warren, Burton Lane, Albert Hague, Cy Coleman, David Lahm, and Quincy Jones.

Deanna Durbin and Vincent Price in the film
version of the Fields-Romberg *Up in Central Park*

CLOSE AS PAGES IN A BOOK

My joy in loving you is past
   understanding;
It makes me much too eager,
   much too demanding.
I'm a very selfish lover with a
   jealous heart.
If you're across the room, I'd be
   alone
I've got to feel your cheek
   against my own.

We'll be close as pages in a
   book,
My love and I.
So close, we can share a single
   look,
Share every sigh.

So close, that before I hear your
   laugh,
My laugh breaks through;
And when a tear starts to appear,
My eyes grow misty too.

Our dreams won't come tumbling
   to the ground,
We'll hold them fast.
Darling, as the strongest book is
   bound,
We're bound to last.
Your life is my life
And while life beats away in my
   heart
We'll be close as pages in a book,
Never to part.

Face It. Joe Fields was back in New York again, having become (after years of churning out studio scripts in semi-anonymity) a tremendously successful Broadway playwright, coauthoring, with his old Hollywood writing partner Jerome Chodorov, the comedy *My Sister Eileen.* Opening in 1940, it was a monster hit, running more than two years, and they followed it up with *Junior Miss,* which ran almost as long.

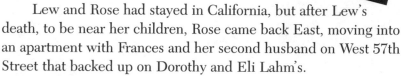

Lew and Rose had stayed in California, but after Lew's death, to be near her children, Rose came back East, moving into an apartment with Frances and her second husband on West 57th Street that backed up on Dorothy and Eli Lahm's.

Like almost everyone else she knew during the war, Dorothy had put in her time working at the Stage Door Canteen, where theatre celebrities and others dished up food, hospitality and entertainment to visiting servicemen. One evening in August of 1945, she was out with friends and heard a woman from Travelers Aid talking about a young soldier she'd encountered at Penn Station, his chest covered with sharpshooting medals, and his arms filled with dolls that he'd just won by putting his skill to work at a Coney Island shooting gallery.

Dorothy had been slated to come up with another project for Merman. Sitting there listening to the woman's story, her next thought came to her fully formed, in a flash: Ethel Merman as Annie Oakley. "It was the only time in my life an idea came absolutely from God," she would say later. The next day she got on the phone to Merman, who was in Doctors' Hospital recovering two days after the cesarean birth of her son, and Dorothy told her she had an idea that couldn't wait. Arriving at her friend's bedside, she said, "Mermsie—want to be Annie Oakley?" Merman was thrilled. Dorothy and Herb first took the idea to Mike Todd, whose reaction was "Who's gonna care about a girl who knows from nothing but guns?," and he passed on the project. That afternoon Dorothy ran into Oscar Hammerstein at a Dramatists Guild luncheon (sometimes it's an ASCAP luncheon; the story varies, like *Rashomon*), and afterward she took him aside and said, "What do you think of Ethel

Merman as Annie Oakley?" He loved it, and told her to come back to the office with him so they could talk to Rodgers.

Rodgers and Hammerstein had just three years beforehand become a team and created a sensation with *Oklahoma!* When Dorothy found herself in their offices discussing *Annie Oakley*, as the show was to be called, it had been a scant three months since they had again stunned Broadway, this time with *Carousel*. It was never really a question of Rodgers and Hammerstein writing the Annie Oakley show; they had taken a completely different direction with their first two collaborations, so that an old-fashioned musical comedy wasn't their kind of thing. They had, however, started producing shows when they weren't writing them. When Dorothy once more blurted out her one-line idea, the answer from her old childhood crush came back just as fast: "You write it, we'll do it."

Herb and Dorothy went to work writing the book, which included some song titles, as Dorothy, naturally, was to write the lyrics as well. The first choice of composer was obvious, from both Dorothy's and Hammerstein's point of view. It had to be Jerome Kern. Kern hadn't done a Broadway show since *Very Warm for May* some six years before, and he had in the interim suffered two more strokes, from which he'd recovered, and was in fairly good health. When the script was finished, Rodgers (who'd regarded Kern as an idol since his boyhood trips to the Princess Theatre shows) mailed it off to Kern and wired, "It would be one of the greatest honors in my life if you would consent to write the music for this show."

Kern was enthusiastic. He'd been missing Broadway—both the work and the stature a composer in the theatre held, compared with the lack of control and low position on the totem pole that creative people traded for the fat Hollywood paychecks. (However, he had recently done scores for two Rita Hayworth films, *You Were Never Lovelier*, collaborating with Johnny Mercer, and *Cover Girl*, with Ira Gershwin, that yielded two of his most famous standards, "I'm Old Fashioned" and "Long Ago and Far Away." He'd also won a second Academy Award, with Hammerstein, for "The Last Time I Saw Paris.")

To help get him east, Hammerstein added an enticing plan for a big revival of *Show Boat*. By the beginning of November, Jerry and Eva Kern were in New York, settling into an apartment at the St. Regis Hotel. Kern was delighted to be back in his hometown, eager to begin the work at hand, and already checking on the costume designs for *Show Boat*. On the morning of Monday, November 5, 1946, he left the St. Regis, after leaving a note in soap on the bathroom mirror to remind Eva of her lunch date with Dorothy. Walking down the block on his way to shop for antiques, he suddenly collapsed on the corner of 57th Street and Park Avenue, while waiting for a light. The police and ambulance arrived to find that he was carrying no identification, and they took him to the city hospital on Welfare Island, where, anonymous, he was placed in the charity ward, surrounded by indigents and derelicts.

However, somebody had noticed the pin in his lapel, which bore the ASCAP emblem (the story sometimes goes that he had a lone ASCAP card in his pocket), and though "ASCAP" didn't mean much to the authorities, they placed a call to the organization, who identified Kern and immediately located Oscar Hammerstein at a Dramatists Guild meeting. Hammerstein, Dorothy, and Eva Kern were at his bedside as soon as they could get there. But though Kern regained consciousness briefly, he had suffered another stroke, and soon lapsed into a coma. He held on for a few days, during which time they had him moved to Doctors' Hospital (where just a few months before, Dorothy had told Merman of the Oakley plans). Hammerstein and Dorothy, as well as Eva and Betty Kern, were given rooms nearby so they could keep a bedside vigil. Kern slipped away on the afternoon of November 11, while Hammerstein was at his side (Hammerstein had even lifted the oxygen tent and softly sung to him, "I've Told Ev'ry Little Star," which Kern loved, trying for a response). Dorothy (like Hammerstein) was inconsolable. She had lost not only an artistic alter ego and partner, but a mentor and soulmate.

When the shock had subsided and they met to decide what would become of *Annie Oakley*, discussions began about what composer they could bring in to replace Kern—something none of them liked to think about, and something they knew few composers would presume to do. Irving Berlin was immediately discounted, because not only did he work exclusively on projects he produced himself, he always wrote both music and lyrics—and Dorothy was already the show's lyricist. As other names were tossed around, Hammerstein protested that they at least owed it to themselves to let Berlin turn them down; how would they know unless they at least asked?

Sensitive to the fact that should Berlin accept, it would displace Dorothy from a project that had been her idea in the first place, Dick and Oscar put the decision to Dorothy, who gamely agreed that if they could get Irving Berlin, it would be worth it to her to gladly step aside.

With her motherhood of the Annie Oakley project and her work on it to date, Dorothy's concession has to be looked at as one of considerable grace. On the other hand, it is also very likely that under the impact of Kern's death, the concept of going on to write the *Annie* lyrics without him and with a replacement was disheartening; it may have been easier for her to let the whole thing go than it would under normal circumstances.

In any case, Berlin, doubtful about the whole idea (let alone the prospect of replacing Kern), read Herb and Dorothy's book and liked it, but still didn't think the subject matter suited him. However, he took the script away with him to Atlantic City for the weekend, and when he came back, it was with three songs and tremendous enthusiasm. The songs, "You Can't Get a Man with a Gun," "There's No Business Like Show Business," and "Doin' What Comes Natur'lly," had been inspired so directly from the book (including Dorothy's song titles), Berlin maintained, that he wanted to acknowledge the credit that he owed the Fieldses. Therefore, in an extremely unusual move, Berlin assigned Dorothy and Herb, as the book's authors, a full fifty percent of the rights to the show. According to standard practice, the Fieldses were entitled to one-third as librettists; Berlin, to one-third as composer, plus another

third as the lyricist. The action was particularly striking in view of Berlin's reputation as a
shrewd businessman and protector of his
own interests.

Berlin, more legendary for his individual songs than for his scores for musicals, completed the remainder of the
numbers quickly; according to a well-
known story, he wrote "Anything You
Can Do" in a taxicab on the way home
from the meeting in Hammerstein's living
room where they had decided on the need for such a
challenge song.

Dorothy and Herb's book gave Ethel Merman the best star
entrance she ever had—coming on immediately after shooting a
bird off the hat of a woman onstage. The book chronicled the
escapades of the legendary (though clunky) gal sharpshooter who
emerged from the hills to become a star of Buffalo Bill Cody's Wild
West Show and her moonstruck pursuit of the show's other star,
Frank Butler (played by Ray Middleton). It was the best libretto
they'd ever produced. Solid, colorful, and integrated in the way the
songs were allowed to further character and story, it had both
laughs and poignant moments. "We did a lot of research on Annie
Oakley and Frank Butler," Dorothy said later, "and both of them
apparently were about the dullest people in the world. Annie
Oakley in real life used to sit in her tent and *knit*, for God's sake."
As the libretto needed to do most, it showcased to the hilt the formidable talents of its star. It was the fifth show the Fieldses and
Merman had done together (and for Merman, the fifth in a row).

Though it may have been an idea that came directly from God,
it also benefited from the work of Miss Fields's subconscious: in
1935 Joe Fields had written a screenplay (though other writers
eventually got the final credit) for RKO called *Annie Oakley*, which
had been made into a movie starring Barbara Stanwyck. A decade
later, when the musical's libretto was finished and the creative team

Ethel Merman, the inspiration for *Annie Get Your Gun* and for many, *the*
Annie Oakley. But if everyone thought that the show could only be carried by
The Merm, they were wrong. Many have successfully recreated the part. It
would become librettist Dorothy Fields's most resounding stage success

decided to spruce up the title, Dorothy suggested *Annie Get Your Gun*. She didn't have to look much further than the original title for her last Merman show, *Something for the Boys*—which, before Mike Todd had it changed, was *Jenny Get Your Gun*.

Once again, as with *Stars in Your Eyes* six years earlier, Dorothy found herself working with director Josh Logan, whom Rodgers and Hammerstein had called in on the project about the same time Logan was being released from wartime army service overseas. Just as Logan had used his psychology on Dorothy and Arthur Schwartz during *Stars in Your Eyes* to convince them to discard "My New Kentucky Home," so it was at his insistence that at the end of the show, Annie Oakley wins the heart of Frank Butler by purposely losing the shooting contest between them. It would, he maintained, give Annie some needed character growth. Unlike *Stars in Your Eyes*, this time it worked, dramatically (though hardly striking a blow for the women's movement).

As remembered later by the principal parties involved, from the producers to the director and composer, librettists, star, and cast, the production process of *Annie Get Your Gun* was among the most pleasant working experiences of their careers. There was no dissension to speak of, no bickering, ego flexing, or power grapples; no painful, hysterical, wee-hour rewrite sessions, or dress rehearsal crises—none of the standard vicissitudes of work on a Broadway musical. Everything went so smoothly that from start to finish, it seemed right, natural, and blessed, and by the time the show was ready to open its pre-Broadway tryout in New Haven, the only person who didn't share the general euphoria that had settled over the participants was Josh Logan, recently recovered from a nervous breakdown and waiting for the proverbial other shoe to drop.

From the first moment of the New Haven run, there was no reason to worry. The audience's reception was as ecstatic as any in memory, from the opening laughs to the deafening applause as,

Mary Martin as Annie in the national tour, 1947–49

number after number, Irving Berlin's songs stopped the show: the Merman numbers "Doin' What Comes Natur'lly," "You Can't Get a Man With a Gun," "Moonshine Lullaby," "I Got Lost in His Arms," "I Got the Sun in the Morning," "I'm an Indian Too"; Ray Middleton singing "I'm a Bad, Bad Man," "The Girl That I Marry," and "My Defenses Are Down"; the duets "They Say It's Wonderful" and "Anything You Can Do," and the rousing inauguration of the entertainers' anthem, "There's No Business Like Show Business."

When the giddy creators and company arrived in New York for the April 25 opening, the first thing that happened was that during the load-in of Jo Mielziner's scenery at the Imperial Theatre, a girder tore loose from its anchoring, taking down with it part of a brick wall. Though nobody was hurt (it could have been disastrous had it occurred with the cast onstage), the theatre was immediately closed down for repairs and the Broadway opening postponed. In the interim, the Shuberts found a booking in Philadelphia for the ready-to-go company. On May 16, with the repairs made, *Annie Get Your Gun* opened in New York.

The glittering first-night audience was filled with the usual celebrities and VIPs, and as the cast launched into the material that, from its out-of-town try-outs, was already tinged with the aura of surefire success, an interesting thing happened. Nothing. The jokes got barely a laugh, as did Merman's clowning and "goon look" (her limp, lovestruck reaction to Frank Butler), and Berlin's show stopping songs received polite smatterings of applause. Rodgers, Hammerstein, Logan, Berlin, Herb, and Dorothy were all seized by the same mixture of panic and nausea.

When the first act was over and the audience congregated at intermission, Merman was explaining to Josh Logan that she had gotten through the first half of the show by thinking "Screw you, you jerks, if you were as good as I am, you'd be up here." But during the interval, the peculiar chemistry of audiences (especially opening night audiences) was at work, and through their buzz, interaction, and mutual vibrations, they "decided" that they liked it.

Lily Fayol, looking exceedingly French, in *Annie du Far West*, the Gallic version, Paris, 1950

Returning for the second half, which opened with Merman and the ensemble singing "I Got Lost in His Arms," suddenly they were responsive, laughing at the jokes, appreciative of the songs. Somewhere between the end of the first and beginning of the second acts, *Annie Get Your Gun* had become a Broadway hit. It would go on to run a gargantuan 1,147 performances, only the second musical (after *Oklahoma!*) to break the 1,000 show mark.

Still, when the reviews appeared, everyone involved with *Annie* was shocked to find that with the exception of raves for Ethel Merman, the show received a large dose of lukewarm, qualified critical notices. Merman was universally praised for her showmanship, prowess as a comedienne, and just plain lung power. The show got this: "Irving Berlin's score is musically not exciting—of the real songs, only one or two are tuneful . . ." (Kronenberger, *PM*); "The book is on the flimsy side. And rather witless, too . . . Irving Berlin's score is not a notable one . . ." (Morehouse, *Sun*); ". . . it isn't the greatest show in the world" (Chapman, *Daily News*); and "an agreeable evening on the town" (Nichols, *New York Times*). Though on balance the reviews were favorable because of the credit given to Merman, the experience led to Irving Berlin's oft-quoted remark, "Critics—it's a good thing they only write *about* shows and don't actually write them."

Audiences, on the other hand, made *Annie Get Your Gun* one of the most stalwart fixtures of the American musical theatre, effectively as prominent and durable as *Oklahoma!* or *The King and I*. Its score would also be considered Irving Berlin's most significant and enduring work, with practically every song becoming a standard.

With the show's significant financial success, the material rewards were no small matter, particularly with Dorothy and Herb's enlarged 50 percent stake in the royalties. *Annie Get Your Gun*'s film rights were sold to Hollywood for $650,000, to that date the highest price ever paid for the rights to a musical, topping even *Easter Parade*. Ethel Merman, as happened in many stage to screen transfers, would not get to recreate her role onscreen

Lucie Arnaz and Harve Presnell, the Jones Beach Theater, 1978

(similarly the biggest disappointment of her career would come when her Mamma Rose in *Gypsy* was given to Rosalind Russell). MGM's Arthur Freed had bought *Annie* for Judy Garland. Shooting began, but Garland was going through a period of extreme mental difficulty, and was unable to function. The existing footage, which shows an impaired and disoriented Garland, was unusable, and she was replaced by Betty Hutton, with whom they completed the picture, released in 1950. In fact, virtually nobody from the stage production was involved in the Hollywood rendition (the screenplay was written by Sidney Sheldon).

The stage version seemed to have an indefinite life of its own. If people thought (as the creators once did) that only Merman would be able to play Annie Oakley, they were surprised when Mary Martin took the show on an enormously successful national tour, and Dolores Gray had a similar success in London. Even today, though the book (always a solid, old-fashioned confection) has dated the way other star vehicles of the period have, *Annie Get Your Gun* ranks in the top five musicals licensed every year by the

ANNIE GET YOUR GUN

SYNOPSIS OF SCENES

ACT I.

Scene 1: The Wilson House, a summer hotel on the outskirts of Cincinnati, Ohio. July

Scene 2: A Pullman Parlor in an Overland Steam Train. Six weeks later.

Scene 3: The Fair Grounds at Minneapolis, Minn. A few days later.

Scene 3a: The Arena of the Big Tent.

Scene 4: A Dressing-room Tent. The same day.

Scene 5: The Arena of the Big Tent. Later that night.

ACT II.

Scene 1: The Deck of a Cattle Boat. Eight months later.

Scene 2: Ballroom of the Hotel Brevoort. The next night.

Scene 3: Aboard a Ferry. Enroute to Governor's Island. Next morning.

Scene 4: Governor's Island. Near the Fort. Immediately following.

MUSICAL NUMBERS

ACT I.

Buffalo Bill . . . . .Charlie and Ensemble

I'm a Bad, Bad Man . . . . .Frank and Girls

Danced by Duncan Noble, Paddy Stone,
Parker Wilson, and Ensemble

Doin' What Comes Naturally . . . . .Annie, Sisters, Brother and Foster Wilson

The Girl That I Marry . . . . .Frank

You Can't Get a Man With a Gun . . . . .Annie

Show Business . . . . .Buffalo Bill, Charlie, Frank and Annie

They Say It's Wonderful . . . . .Frank and Annie

Moonshine Lullaby . . . . .Annie and Trio

I'll Share It All With You . . . . .Winnie and Tommy

"Ballyhoo" . . . . .Danced by Riding Mistress and Show People

Reprise: Show Business . . . . .Annie

My Defenses Are Down . . . . .Frank and Boys

Wild Horse Ceremonial Dance . . . . .The Wild Horse,
Braves and Maidens

I'm an Indian Too . . . . .Annie

Adoption Dance . . . . .Annie, The Wild Horse and Braves

ACT II

Lost in His Arms . . . . .Annie and Ensemble

Who Do You Love, I Hope? . . . . .Winnie and Tommy
Danced by Winnie, Tommy and Ensemble

Sun in the Morning . . . . .Annie and Ensemble
Danced by Roudenko, Nagrin and Show People

Reprise: They Say It's Wonderful . . . . .Annie and Frank

Reprise: The Girl That I Marry . . . . .Frank

Anything You Can Do . . . . .Annie and Frank

Reprise: Show Business . . . . .Entire Company

Rodgers and Hammerstein office (with *Oklahoma!, The Sound of Music, South Pacific*, and *The King and I*). In 1966 a major revival at Lincoln Center saw Ethel Merman, age fifty-eight, take up the role she originated, to tremendous critical and popular acclaim.

For Dorothy, who'd seen her idea take shape under the cloud of Kern's death and her own abdication as the show's lyricist, any lingering shred of disappointment was dispelled by the show's success. The *Annie Get Your Gun* libretto is the Broadway contribution (with *Sweet Charity*) for which she is most remembered.

Dolores Gray, London, 1947

T WOULD BE many years before Dorothy would have a
Broadway hit approaching the magnitude of *Annie Get Your Gun*.
It would also be several before she'd have one that was artistical-
ly satisfying. *Arms and the Girl*, which ushered in the 1950s,
seemed like a good idea to begin with. It was to be a musical version of the play *The Pursuit of Happiness*, written by Lawrence
Langner and his wife, Armina Marshall, under the pseudonyms
Alan Child and Isabelle Louden. Langner and Marshall were
founders of the Theatre Guild and the driving force behind it, and
had originally presented the play in 1934. The comedy, set during
the American Revolution, dealt with a Hessian soldier who falls in
love with a strong-willed colonial girl. It saw a sprightly run of 248
performances, and the following year was made into a movie with
Joan Bennett.

A decade and a half later, the Theatre
Guild was grappling with lean times (despite
the fact that it had produced both
Oklahoma! and *Carousel* several years earlier). Langner spoke with Dorothy and Herb
about turning their old reliable into a
musical, and the production was planned.
Rouben Mamoulian, who'd directed
Oklahoma! and *Carousel*, was hired to
direct; Dorothy was, in addition to the
libretto, to do lyrics; and as the composer, they secured the services of Burton
Lane. Lane and Dorothy had been good friends since
Hollywood days, when he was writing hit songs for the movies.
When he signed to do *Arms and the Girl*, he was just coming off his
enormous success with *Finian's Rainbow*. But *Arms* was already in
trouble, because Dorothy and Herb couldn't seem to mold the play
into a shape that would support its musicalization. In their repeated
tries to fix its problems, they kept the original main characters and
threw out most of the play, devising their own plot to say in musical
terms what Langner and Marshall had said in more subtle dramatic
ones. The result was problematic, and it didn't seem to want to get
better.

Burton Lane came in from California, and arrived at Dorothy and Eli's gracious country home in Brewster, New York. The idea was that in the country they would be able to relax and begin attacking the show in an informal setting. (Herb was also there, as it was where he and Dorothy did much of their work.) Dorothy, always an enthusiastic hostess, arranged dinner and they sat around amiably until Lane, tired from the trip, excused himself to retire to his room. On his way up, Dorothy gave him a copy of the script, which he read before turning in. He later recalled that he woke up in the middle of the night with the realization that he had to find a way to get out of the project. His dilemma, obviously, was his affection for and close friendship with Dorothy. But he told them that he honestly thought the script was inadequate, and he left the project.

With all parties getting nervous in the face of the looming production schedule, Rouben Mamoulian went to work with Dorothy and Herb, and Morton Gould was hired to replace Lane and write the score. Gould, however, was really a Classical composer and arranger, though with a popular sensibility. He'd only done one musical in the past, *Billion Dollar Baby* (five years earlier, with Comden and Green, Jerome Robbins, and George Abbott, following up *On the Town*), and while not an abject failure, it had been more ambitious than successful; its mixed reviews had fingered Gould's music as not particularly melodious. Michael Kidd was brought in to choreograph the dances.

Nanette Fabray was cast as the feisty New Englander Jo Kirkland, who dresses in a militia uniform and takes up arms to whup the British, in the process discovering Georges Guetary as the Hessian deserter Franz von Schilling, taking him for a spy, and falling in love with him. There were its fun moments, like Fabray doing a colonial striptease, and the adaptation of the original play's bundling scene (after the old New England custom whereby a courting couple would get into a specal bed together, fully dressed,

Georges Guetary and Nanette Fabray getting help arming themselves in preparation for *Arms and the Girl*, for which Dorothy collaborated with Morton Gould

Nanette Fabray and Georges Guetary in *Arms and the Girl*'s bundling scene

under a lot of blankets and separated by a board). There were songs like "That's My Fella" and "He Will Tonight," and the ambitiously constructed "I Like It Here," sung by Franz. Pearl Bailey stole the show as a runaway slave named Connecticut (the only character not appearing in the original show; the reason she's called "Connecticut" is that she's no longer in Virginia, which used to be her name). Bailey was given the two most memorable songs— "Nothin' for Nothin,'" a hummable tune with a "folksy" dialect lyric and a verse that begins:

> No bird ever caught a worm by sticking his nose
>   in the air
> He gotta scratch and dig all day
> Dem worms don't jes' throw themselves away,
>   ye know!

And "There Must Be Something Better Than Love," tailored for Bailey, with a sophisticated lyric much more typical of Dorothy's style:

> There must be something better than love
> There must be something better in view
> But if there is something better than love,
> Who wants it? Do you?

(A decade and a half later, *Sweet Charity* would have a similarly titled song, "There's Gotta Be Something Better than This.")

Though Dorothy produced some nice lyrics for the show, the initial problems with developing the book were only compounded by the plot contrivances, unlikely incongruities (the slave Connecticut sings in dialect the first time, but not the second), and characterizations that sometimes led to unintentional humor.

Perhaps Dorothy's most unfortunate moment as lyricist came in her attempt to give Franz an earnest, homey vehicle to express his yearnings: to a lovely Gould melody, she wrote, "A Cow and a Plough and a Frau." Dorothy, of course, had about as much bucolic sense as Auntie Mame. Oscar Hammerstein was good at writing about grass and trees and corn and such things, which he did with convincing, moving simplicity. Dorothy's hallmark was also simplicity, and like Hammerstein she was direct and colloquial, but her brand of simplicity had an innately urban ring closer to Larry Hart's. Anyone looking randomly at the song title would naturally assume "A Cow and a Plough and a Frau" was a springboard for the Fields wit. Instead, she writes:

> Dreams about a meadow, rolling in the sunlight
> And a field of clover for the pretty cow

Arms and the Girl opened at the 46th Street Theatre on February 2, 1950. The critics were varied in their reactions, giving nice notices to Fabray and particularly Bailey, but most agreeing that the show didn't work. At worst, George Jean Nathan called the libretto "witless" and the score one "that goes in one ear, which has heard most of it before, and then inconveniently refuses to go out the other." At best, William Hawkins of the *World Telegram & Sun* summed it up: "You can stash *Arms and the Girl* somewhere between the bottom of the top drawer and the top of the second. It misses being real class of the ever-memorable kind because of the corrugated aspect of its fun. When it is good it is rip-roaring musical comedy . . . . Between stuff like this and the pretty wonderful dances there are moments that just plain thud." The show ran 134 performances—limping through a little over four months—and then closed, losing money.

However, Dorothy would follow up the *Arms and the Girl* debacle with one of her greatest artistic achievements in the the-

ARMS AND THE GIRL

MUSICAL NUMBERS

ACT I.

"A Girl With a Flame" ....Jo

"That's What I Told Him Last Night" ....Aaron and Girls

"I Like It Here" ....Franz

"That's My Fella"

    Song ....Jo

    Dance ....Arthur Partington and Barbara McCutcheon

and

    First two couples ...Fern Whitney, Maria Harrington, William Inglis, Edmund Balin

    Whittler and Girl ....Marc West, Annabelle Gold

    Deacon ....Lou Yetter

    Siren ....Onna White

    Butterfly Catcher ....Peter Genaro
    and Girl ....Patricia Muller

    The Pursued ....Robert Josias

    Patient One ....Shirley Robbins

"A Cow, a Plough and a Frau" ....Franz

"Nothin' for Nothin'" ....Connecticut

"He Will Tonight" ....Jo and Girls

"Plantation in Philadelphia"

    Song ....Jo, Franz, Connecticut, Sherwood and Company

    Dance ....Boys and Girls

"You Kissed Me" ....Jo

ACT II

"Don't Talk" (Reprise) ....Sherwood

"I'll Never Learn" ....Jo and Franz

"There Must Be Something Better Than Love" ....Connecticut

"She's Exciting" ....Franz

"Mister Washington! Uncle George!" ....The Boys and Girls

"A Cow, a Plough and a Frau" (Reprise) ....Jo and Franz

atre, the musical adaptation of Betty Smith's novel *A Tree Grows in Brooklyn*. The 1943 bestseller had been based on the author's childhood experiences in the borough across the bridge. The show was produced by George Abbott, who also directed and coauthored the libretto, helping Betty Smith adapt her novel for the stage.

At the time, the austere Abbott had been a Broadway professional for almost forty years, having made his debut as an actor in 1913, at age 26. He'd started directing and producing plays in the 1920s, moving to musicals and an association with Rodgers and Hart in 1935 when he staged *Jumbo*; they went on to collaborate on *On Your Toes*, *The Boys from Syracuse*, and *Pal Joey*. Having pioneered the modern musical comedy, Abbott was the master of stagecraft and timing and had an uncanny instinct about what made a show work. Dry and forbidding, he was a proponent of good, clean fun, and he balanced the stoicism of his Scottish heritage with a passion for tennis and ballroom dancing. His protégés included Jerome Robbins, Bob Fosse, and most notably Hal Prince, who was his assistant, then longtime associate. Often undertaking two or even three shows a season, Abbott intimidated generations of actors, who called him "Mister Abbott"; he offered them his inimitable brand of communication, like his fabled answer to the actor who asked what his motivation for a particular line was: "Your paycheck."

By *A Tree Grows in Brooklyn* in 1951, he was perceived as the grand master of "good old-fashioned" musical comedy, having been overtaken in the pioneering role by the musical theatre of Rodgers and Hammerstein. Abbott, however, continued to dominate that still-thriving branch of Broadway with its own distinct lineage of classic musicals that, despite the arrival of *Oklahoma!*, would include *On the Town*, *High Button Shoes*, *Where's Charley?*, *Call Me Madam*, *Wonderful Town*, *The Pajama Game*, *Damn Yankees*, *Once Upon a Mattress*, and *Fiorello!* (all of which were under his tutelage), as well as *Bells Are Ringing*, *Silk Stockings*, *Guys and Dolls*, *Can-Can*, *The Music Man*, and *How to Succeed in Business Without Really Trying* (many of them guided by protégés like Robbins and Fosse).

Actually, *A Tree Grows in Brooklyn* was a musical play, much closer in feeling to a Rodgers and Hammerstein show than, say, *Call Me Madam*, in which Abbott had just steered Irving Berlin and Ethel Merman to a successful *Annie Get Your Gun* follow-up. Just as Betty Smith's novel was a very real and poignant story of a family's struggle, so the play recounted the tale of the charming, alcoholic ne'er-do-well Johnny Nolan, whose wife and daughter are ultimately unable to head him off from tragedy. In this, the show was and still is compared to *Carousel*.

A Tree Grows in Brooklyn had a warm and sentimental turn-of-the-century aura. It was, in fact, Dorothy's fourth consecutive period show—a trend that would continue until *Sweet Charity*. Once again, a dozen years after *Stars in Your Eyes*, Dorothy was working with her friend Arthur Schwartz (an experience she would always refer to as "pure delight"). Schwartz, one of the major composers in American popular and show music, had begun in the 1920s, a contemporary of the Gershwins, Rodgers, Hart, and Porter. (He wrote songs at summer camp with Hart.) With lyricist Howard Dietz, his most frequent partner, he had his first success, the revue *The Little Show* in 1929.

From there, he went on to help define the sophisticated wit and style of his era, with revues like *The Band Wagon* and *Flying Colors*, which included the songs "I Guess I'll Have to Change My Plan," "Dancing in the Dark," "Louisiana Hayride," "I Love Louisa" and "Alone Together." Splitting in the late '30s with Dietz, who became a Hollywood executive, Schwartz went on to work with an assortment of collaborators, including (apart from Dorothy) Oscar Hammerstein, Ira Gershwin, and Frank Loesser; occasionally he reunited with Dietz. Like Dorothy, who also had a string of collaborators, Arthur Schwartz enjoys less name recognition with the general public than his accomplishments deserve. Unlike Dorothy, he continued to devote much of his stage work to revues—which, though they produced memorable standard songs, vanished when they finished running, not permitting him to be identified with

Shirley Booth as Aunt Cissy in *A Tree Grows in Brooklyn*

Shirley Booth with Johnny Johnston, *A Tree Grows in Brooklyn*

revivable shows. *A Tree Grows in Brooklyn* allowed him to sink his exceptional melodic gifts into a substantial vehicle.

The libretto for *A Tree Grows in Brooklyn*, which tried to circumvent the basic sadness of the story, focused on the irresponsible dreamer Johnny (the novel's story had been told from the point of view of his daughter). Then the writers fashioned the female star part not for Katie Nolan, the stoic wife, but for her sister, the lovably blowzy, aging good-time gal Cissy—cast brilliantly with Shirley Booth.

Booth, who became known to households worldwide as TV's Hazel, had just the year before won both the Tony and the Oscar for her performance in *Come Back, Little Sheba*. A native of New York City, Booth possessed both the perfect Brooklynese speech and flawless comic timing for the occasion. "Whenever there was a laugh to be got from a line," Dorothy later recalled, "brother, she got it." The rest of the cast included Johnny Johnston, Marcia Van Dyke as Katie, and Nathaniel Frey as Booth's latest "husband."

Of writing the lyrics for the show, Dorothy said, "The characters told me what I should write—I didn't tell them." What she and Schwartz wrote was her best musical theatre score to date, and arguably the finest of her career. Though a rather schizophrenic amalgam of comic and tragic, the libretto offered a period, Brooklyn-Irish milieu that was perfect for Dorothy's sensibility. The characters had a gentle Damon Runyonesque quality that lent itself to her ear for quirky, slangy speech. Her lyrics were straight-ahead, without a lot of verbal tricks, in the plainspoken vernacular of the people she was writing about.

Perhaps liberated by leaving the libretto chores to someone else, in *A Tree Grows in Brooklyn* Dorothy's songwriting talents and particular ability to create theatre lyrics came together absolutely, for the first time since she had returned to Broadway and taken a new direction. The songs expressed the characters' inner thoughts in their own voices, and their expressions rang true. The opening production number, "Mine 'Til Monday," establishes the Saturday-night tone of the neighborhood, the working-class people who inhabit it, and Johnny Nolan talking about the joys of getting his watch out of the pawnshop for the weekend, only to have it go back again on Monday. "Look Who's Dancing" also exuded a boisterous period flavor.

The score had two ballads that would become standards: "I'll Buy You a Star," in which the unrealistic Johnny promises his wife everything, up to and including the moon, and the torch ballad "Make the Man Love Me," in which Katie expresses her need and willingness to love him unconditionally. "Make the Man Love Me" is among the best songs of Dorothy's career.

A TREE GROWS IN BROOKLYN

MUSICAL NUMBERS

ACT ONE

"Payday" . . . . .The Company

"Mine 'Til Monday" . . . . .Johnny Johnston, Dody Heath and Company

Reprise: . . . . .Jordan Bentley, Dody Heath, Lou Wills, Jr., Joe Calvan, Billy Parsons

"Make the Man Love Me" . . . . .Marcia Van Dyke and Johnny Johnston

"I'm Like a New Broom" . . . . .Johnny Johnston and Friends

"I'm Like a New Broom" reprise . . . . . . .Johnny Johnston and Friends

"Look Who's Dancing" . . . . .Marcia Van Dyke, Shirley Booth, Johnny Johnston, Joe Calvan, Billy Parsons, Lou Wills, Jr. and Doris Wright, Mary Statz, Dorothy Hill

"Love Is the Reason" . . . . .Shirley Booth and Claudia Campbell, Dody Heath, Beverly Purvin, Eleanor Williams

"Mine Next Monday" . . . . .Jordan Bentley and Dody Heath

"If You Haven't Got a Sweetheart" . . . .Delbert Anderson and Company

"I'll Buy You a Star" . . . . .Johnny Johnston and Company

ACT TWO

"That's How It Goes" . . . . .Harland Dixon, Patti Milligan, Janet Parker and Company

"He Had Refinement" . . . . .Shirley Booth

"Growing Pains" .Johnny Johnston, Nomi Mitty

"Is That My Prince?" . . . . .Shirley Booth, Albert Linville

"Halloween" . . . . .Johnny Johnston, Lou Wills, Jr., Joe Calvan, Billy Parsons and Dancers, Children and Singers

"Don't Be Afraid" . . . . .Johnny Johnston

"I'm Like a New Broom" reprise . . . . .Johnny Johnston

"Love Is the Reason" . . . . .Shirley Booth and Nat Frey

"Look Who's Dancing" reprise . . . . .Nat Frey and Children

"If You Haven't Got a Sweetheart" . . . . .The Company

But mainly the show belonged to Shirley Booth's raucous and ribald Cissy. The pleasure that Dorothy took in writing for Cissy's personality is obvious, and her lyrics precisely capture the style and rhythm of the character's speech, particularly in two of the show's strongest numbers, "Love Is the Reason" and "He Had Refinement." ("'He Had Refinement' is my favorite Fields lyric," says lyricist Fred Ebb. "It is brilliantly comic and totally in character. Every word is a model of brilliant construction and each stanza leads to an appropriate and hilarious punchline. I think it is one of the finest musical comedy songs in all musical comedy literature.") In a soft-shoe tempo Cissy describes her first husband. In writing the lyrics, Dorothy abstained from her own verbal cleverness to achieve a result that is instead funny on a human level:

> He was shy and awfully modest
>   he was so high bred.
> If the wind blew up my bloomers
>   would his face get red!
> He undressed with all the lights off
>   until we was wed.
> He had refinement.

It's a true character lyric, in that there's no question that the view expressed belongs not only to a specific situation, but uniquely to one personality. Listen to the words of "He Had Refinement" and one instantly gets a picture of what Cissy is all about, much as one does with "Adelaide's Lament" in *Guys and Dolls*. "The Way You Look Tonight," or even "A Fine Romance," is not designed to tell much about the singer except for the emotions expressed; they're in the songwriter's voice, and universal. Rather than use fancy rhyme schemes or Cole Porterish gymnastics (incongruous with Brooklynspeak), Dorothy used simple end rhymes, with some unflashy internal rhymes and alliteration (shy/high, blew/bloomers),

DOROTHY'S COLLABORATION WITH ARTHUR SCHWARTZ

on projects like *A Tree Grows in Brooklyn* yielded some of the musical theatre's most elegant contributions. Schwartz's son, the disk jockey and classic pop guru Jonathan Schwartz, remembers, from the viewpoint of a teenager, the lyricist's and composer's relationship as being "exceptionally warm and exceptionally loving." "At the same time, they were wonderful, gossipy chums and literate collaborators," he says. "My father was particularly fond of Dorothy's ability to write comedy numbers, 'He Had Refinement' being a classic example. And he was able to supply her with some really beautiful melodies. Jerome Kern had told my father that when writing a comedy song the melody must be as beautiful as possible, and my father always remembered that. So in *A Tree Grows in Brooklyn* and *By the Beautiful Sea* you'll find some lovely Arthur Schwartz melodies attached to Dorothy's wonderful, warm-spirited, witty lyrics.

"Dorothy had to call herself 'one of the boys.' Those were her words, it was a self-description that went for four decades, 'the boys,' of course, being the other songwriters, because she was the only woman. And that kind of neutralized the fact that she was a woman. I can see her saying it.

"Dorothy was very empathic and sympathetic to a young teenage boy alone, and she was very kind. I always felt Dorothy's warmth toward me. My father and I often took long walks in the city. And whenever we found ourselves in the shadows, one of us would always say, 'Let's cross over to the Dorothy side of the street.'"

HE HAD REFINEMENT

If I ever saw a prince
My Harry was him.
Always smelled from pepper-
    mints.
His person was trim.
His voice was passionate.
Soulful his face was.
He never took no liberties,
He knew what his place was

He'd say par'n my glove, politely
When he shook my hand.
And he'd pass me the evening
    paper
When his soup was fanned.
He only used four-letter words
I didn't understand.
He had refinement.

He would never sit down to eat
Without his shirt was on
Or come out of the bathroom
    dripping
Like a dying swan
Or call a visitor a slob
Until the slob was gone.
He had refinement.

One time he said, may I suggest
You call a lady's chest, a chest,
Instead of her points of interest?
Dainty . . .
Ain't he?

He was shy and awfully modest
He was so high bred.
If the wind blew up my bloomers
Would his face get red!

He undressed with all the
    lights off
Until we was wed.
He had refinement.

He would walk next to the gutter
So I sh'un't get hit.
With a piller he'd kill mosquitos
So I sh'un't get bit.
Only certain kind exertions
For me he'd permit.
He had refinement.

In the water at Coon-y Island
Was our first embrace
When my water wings flew off
And hit him in the face.
He introduced himself before
He put them back in place.
He had refinement.

At Luna Park all night we sat.
Our food got cold, our beer
    got flat.
I knew what he was driving at.
I could-a forbid it—
But I did it.

He had such respect and feeling
All our married life.
Just the thought that maybe he'd
    hurt me
Cut him like a knife
So he never mentioned that
He had another wife.
He had refinement.
Refinement!
A gennel-man to his fingernails
    was he.

FRED EBB: "I THINK DOROTHY FIELDS WAS A GREAT LYRICIST

because of her humanity, her humor, her simplici-ty, and her incredible, meticulous craftsmanship. I don't think you would find a false rhyme or any other kind of lyrical error in any of the many great songs she has written.

"I think she had a particularly feminine voice, and the reason is that I cannot imagine a man writing some of the lyrics for which she is most famous, that is, 'Make the Man Love Me,' 'Pink Taffeta Sample Size 10,' 'Nobody Does it Like Me.' I don't know why this is so—and it could be because when I hear these songs, I know she wrote them—but to me, they sound particularly feminine."

Dorothy and Herb with Shirley Booth

MAKE THE MAN LOVE ME

You kissed me once by mistake,
Thought I was somebody else.
I felt that kiss and I envied
That somebody else.

I wanted you for myself,
I guess I was shameless and
   bold.
But I made a plan in my heart
I've never breathed, I've never
   told.

I must try to make the man love
   me,
Make the man love me now.
Bye and bye, I'll make the man
   happy,
I know how.

He must see how badly I want
   him,
Want him just as he is.
May I say that should the man
   ask me,
I'll be his.

Can I tell the man just how
   dearly blessed we would be.
All the beauty I see so clearly,
Oh why can't he?

So I pray to heaven above me,
Pray until day grows dim,
For a way to make the man
   love me,
As I love him.

and concentrated on building jokes solidly to the payoff. "He Had Refinement" is not only one of Dorothy's finest, it's one of the best lyrics of the genre.

Perfecting the character lyric was something Dorothy had been aspiring to since her flapper days writing revues, when she yearned for more cohesive dramatic vehicles in which every song would count toward an end, and each character's expressions would be completely different from every other's. By the late '40s and early '50s, this was the way most musicals were headed, including more and more seamless transition from dialogue to song. By the time *A Tree Grows in Brooklyn* was written, Dorothy's additional skills as a dramatist had made her one of the leaders (with people like Hammerstein) in evolving the musical show into a true manifestation of the drama.

Opening in New York at the Alvin Theatre on April 19, 1951, *A Tree Grows in Brooklyn* got predominantly rave reviews, with a couple of notices that were less than charmed, and much of the response was a love letter to Shirley Booth. Brooks Atkinson wrote in the *Times*, ". . . *A Tree Grows in Brooklyn* turns out to be one of those happy inspirations that the theatre dotes on. With the richest score Arthur Schwartz has written in years, it opened last evening to begin a long and affectionate career . . . To hear Miss Booth singing 'Love is the Reason' in a sort of comic fugue arrangement is to enjoy musical comedy at its best . . . In short, it's a darlin' of a show. People in Brooklyn ought to be proud."

John Chapman of the *Daily News* wrote, "*A Tree Grows in Brooklyn* is a splendid musical . . . [Shirley Booth] had me weeping with laughter. I had quite a lot of eye trouble last evening. If it wasn't from laughing it was from being deeply moved."

In the *World-Telegram & Sun* William Hawkins wrote, "It is a terribly rare combination of heart and craftsmanship and exquisite taste that makes you love being the target of its emotions. I have rarely had more fun laughing, and never had more fun crying. This is an experience of real honesty, taste and ingenuity. . . ."

Although more than one critic considered it a weakness that it was essentially two shows, one comic and one tragic, the way *A Tree Grows in Brooklyn* had landed led everyone to believe they had a hit. All were surprised and disappointed, therefore, when it failed to ignite and audiences didn't show up in sufficient numbers. Despite the rave reviews, artistic achievement, and Shirley Booth, the show ran less than a year, closing after only 267 performances.

By this time, Dorothy, Eli, and the children had moved from the apartment on West 57th Street to a large flat at 525 Park Avenue. David, who was now ten, had early on shown a musical ability obviously inherited from his mother's side, though it was his father who disciplined him to practice the piano. Eliza, three years younger, would eventually grow up to be an artist. In the fifties, the family split their time between Manhattan and the house in Brewster (some years based completely there), where Dorothy hired an off-duty policeman to drive David down to the Riverdale Country School every morning, while Eliza attended the local public school.

An avid gardener, Dorothy spent a lot of her time in the country tending to her flowers, but when she was not down in the soil in her gardening duds, she was living up to both Dorothy Rodgers and Dorothy Hammerstein's description of her as the most elegant woman they knew. (She favored tailored suits and later on, pants.) Dorothy Rodgers was austere and patrician, with a fondness for puns and anagram puzzles. (She started David on them as a child, and when he hadn't understood, she'd mailed him her completed newspaper.) Her standard wedding gift to her friends' children was the Columbia Encyclopedia, and like the Australian-born Dorothy Hammerstein, she pursued her talent for decorating (she also invented and patented the Jonny Mop). When the Dorothys were not meeting for lunch, it was for charity work; apart from her work with the Girl Scouts, Dorothy Fields devoted particular time to the Federation of Jewish Philanthropies.

Her wardrobe was not the only area in which she exercised her taste. Having been indoctrinated into antiques and collectibles years earlier by Jerry Kern, Dorothy casually collected items like cigarette boxes, blue opaline glass, and teapots.

Like her husband, Eli (and pals Ethel Merman and Irving Berlin), but unlike most of the theatre community, Dorothy was a registered Republican. But though she was featured in Berlin's "I Like Ike" photo opportunities around the piano, and though on the other hand, friends and associates like Yip Harburg and Jerome Chodorov had been blacklisted, Dorothy had always been particularly apolitical, in her work as well as in her opinions. Her party affiliation was as much in deference to her husband (and the fact that she had always been financially successful, so the GOP was a more pragmatic choice) than to any strong political conviction of her own.

Parties not of the political kind were still Dorothy's forte, and they were held at both residences, assembling an A-list assortment from the theatre, music, literary, and social worlds. A group lounging in deck chairs would look down to see champion swimmer and Aquacade star Eleanor Holm (Mrs. Billy Rose) doing laps in the pool; a gathering in the New York apartment would see Ethel Merman getting up to sing after dinner. In fact, getting up to entertain after dinner was a requisite at all Dorothy's parties—everyone had to. (One indelible evening at which the Burton Lanes were present, a timid Shirley Booth was cajoled into getting up to sing a song, only to be followed by Merman, obviously in need of an ego recharge that night, committing the unthinkable and repeating the song in her own rendition, blowing away the competition.) Merman, a onetime secretary at the B-K Vacuum Booster Brake Company before she started on Broadway at the top in *Girl Crazy*, got on tremendously well with Dorothy, who had, in a manner, also started at the top.

Ever the perfect hostess, Dorothy would find out her guests' favorite foods and serve them (there would always be tiny potato pancakes with caviar). When she was a guest, the occasion would be followed up with a lavish gift, from Tiffany's or an equally elegant provenance, and similar courtesies were extended for birthdays or openings. Her warmth and generosity were appreciated by her considerable circle of friends and acquaintances, who at the same time encountered a core of privacy where she always kept her deepest thoughts in reserve.

She continued to work with Herb, often at the Brewster house, and "Uncle Herbie" was a frequent presence in the family, both in the city and the country, where he indoctrinated his young niece with his own love of horses and riding. Though Dorothy would take jobs on her own, Herb had done no work on Broadway between *Arms and the Girl* and the siblings' next collaboration four years later, *By the Beautiful Sea*. (They'd both worked on 1953's *Carnival in Flanders*, with a score by James Van Heusen and Johnny Burke, and along with most of the cast and creative team, were replaced during the process. Fortunately, too—as despite John Raitt and Dolores Gray, the show opened to scathing reviews and closed after six performances.)

In fact, with Herb's less disciplined habits, Dorothy had long been the driving force in the duo's partnership, strong-arming him into getting up as early as she did and to getting to work by eight or eight-thirty in the morning, pulling him through the jobs to finish on time.

Around the time of *A Tree Grows in Brooklyn*, for the first time in more than a decade of being back on Broaday, Dorothy took some movie work. One reason was that the offers to write Broadway shows were no longer coming as frequently as before; economics and new blood were changing all that. She contributed songs to three pictures for MGM in 1951, one each with three of her favorite colleagues, Harold Arlen, Arthur Schwartz, and Harry Warren. Arlen had had most of his success in Hollywood, and as one of the great masters of American popular song, had written myriad standards (often blues-inflected, frequently with Johnny Mercer), from "Ac-cent-tchu-ate the Positive," "Blues in the Night," "One for My Baby," and "Get Happy" to the scores for *The Wizard of Oz* with Yip Harburg and the Judy Garland *A Star Is Born* (1954) with Ira Gershwin. Warren, with his bouncy, rhythmic tunefulness, had also

L to r: Herbert Fields, Morton Gould (the composer of *Arms and the Girl*), and Dorothy

made his fortune writing for the movies, and since the '20s had been writing hits like "About a Quarter to Nine," "Chattanooga Choo Choo," "Jeepers Creepers," "The More I See You," "I Only Have Eyes for You," "On the Atchison, Topeka and the Santa Fe," and the score for *Forty-Second Street*, with "Lullaby of Broadway," "You're Getting to Be a Habit with Me," "Shuffle Off to Buffalo," and the title song. Warren, however, spent his later years feeling distinctly unrecognized for his achievements, and his friends sometimes chided him for his paranoia.

The pictures she'd returned to the West Coast for were all big, Technicolor MGM 1950s musicals, but none was distinctive. *Mr. Imperium* (with Arlen) was a vehicle for Lana Turner (dubbed by Trudy Erwin) and Ezio Pinza, with Marjorie Main, Cedric Hardwicke, Barry Sullivan, and Debbie Reynolds, and was about an exiled king who comes to Hollywood and romances a movie star. It featured the songs "Andiamo" and "My Love an' My Mule." *Excuse My Dust* (with Schwartz) starred Red Skelton and was a pleasant 1890s comedy about a horseless carriage inventor romancing the daughter of the livery stable owner and had songs like "Spring Has

Ezio Pinza and Lana Turner in *Mr. Imperium*, MGM, 1951, Dorothy's first foray back to Hollywood in over a decade

Sprung" and "That's for Children." *Texas Carnival* (with Warren) was an all-star comedy revolving around mistaken identity at the fairgrounds, with Esther Williams, Red Skelton, Howard Keel, Ann Miller, and Keenan Wynn, and included the songs "Young Folks Should Get Married" and "It's Dynamite."

Two years later she went back to do another score with Arlen (for Twentieth Century-Fox), *The Farmer Takes a Wife*, which put Betty Grable on a barge in the Erie Canal in the 1820s. (Co-written by Joe Fields, it was a remake of the 1935 film that introduced Henry Fonda to the screen.) This score contained the one real standard in all these movies, "Today I Love Everybody." But Dorothy found Hollywood so changed since the golden days of the '30s that

Texas Carnival, MGM, 1951. Ann Miller and Esther Williams doing what they do best. Ann Miller in the air . . .

she spent as little time there as she could. "Every place was crowded," she said later. "The traffic in Beverly Hills was as bad as New York City. But the studios were desolate." Another thing that had changed for her was that now, having become thoroughly used to the total involvement of the Broadway process, she found the piecemeal work style and authors' lack of control in the movie business extremely frustrating. "Especially when you have a girl like Betty Grable playing a cook on the Erie Canal," Dorothy would comment later, "and she comes out in pale pink organdy dresses to work on a barge—and you try to write a very sincere story for this little comedienne who is completely unbelievable."

Back on the East Coast, she and Herb wrote the libretto for a follow-up project with Shirley Booth. The show, which placed Booth as an ex-vaudevillian running a boardinghouse in Coney Island called "By the Beautiful Sea," was yet another period comedy. (Burton Lane had originally been signed to do the score, but as

Red Skelton and Sally Forrest in *Excuse My Dust*. Dorothy and Arthur Schwartz provided the score for MGM's ode to the horseless carriage.

... Esther Williams underwater

with *Arms and the Girl*, he bowed out ahead of time. Arthur
Schwartz was hired.) Tailored to the star's comic persona, the
breezy story chronicled Lottie Gibson's entrancement with
Shakespearean actor Dennis Emery (played by Wilbur Evans) when
he arrives as a boarder; complications ensue regarding his ex-wife
and daughter.

Dorothy and Arthur Schwartz turned out a fine, melodic score,
with numbers like "The Sea Song," "Happy Habit" (sung by the legendary jazz singer Mae Barnes as Booth's housekeeper), "More
Love Than Your Love," and another comedy song for Booth (in the

vein of "He Had Refinement"), "I'd Rather Wake Up by Myself."
During production, the show's original director, Charles Walters,
was replaced by Marshall Jamison, and the choreographer, Donald
Saddler by Helen Tamiris (who'd done the dances for *Up in Central
Park*). Opening on April 8, 1954, *By the Beautiful Sea* met with
largely favorable reviews though nothing like the heartfelt appreciation for the much more ambitious *A Tree Grows in Brooklyn*.
Mostly, *By the Beautiful Sea* was a light, pleasant star vehicle
sequel, and again, Booth got all the attention. Despite its lovely,
skillful score, posterity hasn't elevated the show to *Brooklyn*'s

Shirley Booth and Boys, *By the Beautiful Sea*, 1954

BY THE BEAUTIFUL SEA

SYNPOSIS OF SCENES

The action of the play takes place in Coney Island
during the early 1900s.

ACT I

Scene 1: Backyard of Lottie Gibson's Boarding House
"Mona From Arizona" . . . . .Franklin Kennedy, Reid Shelton,
George Lenz, Larry Laurence

"The Sea Song" . . . . .Shirley Booth, Boarders, Neighbors

Scene 2: Seaside Street in Coney Island
"Old Enough to Love" . . . . .Larry Howard

Scene 3: The Midway at Coney Island
"Coney Island Boat" . . . . .Shirley Booth, Robert Jennings, Visitors

(Counter Melody "In the Good Old Summertime"
by Ren Shields and George Evans)

Scene 4: The Old Mill
"Alone Too Long" . . . . .Wilbur Evans

Scene 5: Backyard of Lottie Gibson's Boarding House
"Happy Habit" . . . . .Mae Barnes

Scene 6: Midway at Coney Island
"Good Time Charlie"

Sports . . . . .Male Dancers

Song . . . . .Larry Howard, Eddie Heim, Eddie Roll,
Mary Harmon, Cindy Robbins, Gloria Smith

Spicy Pictures

The Vendor . . . . .Larry Laurence

Wicked Woman . . . . .Sigyn, Lillian Donau, Cathryn Damon

The Iceman . . . . .Arthur Partington, Cordelia Ware

Serpentina Sal . . . . .Gaby Monet

Finale . . . . .Dancing Company

Scene 7: Seaside Street in Coney Island
Reprise: "Good Time Charlie" . . . . .Larry Howard, Eddie Heim,
Eddie Roll, Mary Harmon,
Cindy Robbins, Gloria Smith

Scene 8: Bedroom of Lottie Gibson's Boarding House
"I'd Rather Wake Up by Myself" . . . . .Shirley Booth

SCENE 9: THE PAVILLION OF FUN

"Hooray for George the Third" ....Thomas Gleason,
Libi Staiger, Visitors

ACT II

SCENE 1: THE BACKYARD OF LOTTIE GIBSON'S BOARDING HOUSE

"Hang Up" ....Mae Barnes, Boarders, Neighbors

Reprise: "Alone Too Long" ....Shirley Booth

"More Love than Your Love" ....Wilbur Evans

SCENE 2: STAGE OF THE BRIGHTON BEACH THEATRE

Vaudeville ....Acts on the Bill: 1. The Acrobat;
2. The Three Clowns;
3. A Lady in Red;
4. Butterfly Wings

"Lottie Gibson Specialty" ....Shirley Booth

SCENE 3: DREAMLAND CASINO

"Throw the Anchor Away" ....Mary Harmon, Larry Laurence,
Arthur Partington

Dance ....Gaby Monet, Arthur Partington,
Larry Howard, Rex Cooper, Patrons

Reprise: "More Love than Your Love" ....Wilbur Evans

SCENE 4: LOTTIE'S BEDROOM

Reprise: "Happy Habit" ....Shirley Booth

SCENE 5: SEASIDE STREET IN CONEY ISLAND

Reprise: "Old Enough to Love" ....Larry Howard, Carol Leigh

SCENE 6: DREAMLAND CASINO

Finale ....Entire Company

DOROTHY'S WARM RELATIONSHIP WITH OSCAR HAMMERSTEIN

(or "Ockie," as his dearest friends called him) had begun in their youth and lasted until his death. Since Dorothy Hammerstein (the second of "the three Dorothys") was among Fields's closest friends, they did things like travel cross-country together on the Super Chief, which Jamie Hammerstein, the family's youngest, recalls: "I must have been about five, and we went from New York to LA together. Dorothy loved kids, and she didn't have any of her own until late in life, so she spent time with me, and I can remember how I had nothing but love and affection for her. And on the way, I remember looking out the window at the Atchison, Topeka and the Santa Fe railroad. And I kept saying to myself, 'Atchison, Topeka and the Santa Fe; Atchison, Topeka and the Santa Fe,' in rhythm to the train. And Dorothy said to me, 'Someday you'll be a songwriter.' The odd thing about it is that it became a hit song, but neither of us wrote it."

Betty Grable and Dale Robertson in *The Farmer Takes a Wife*, Twentieth Century-Fox, 1953. Dorothy's second collaboration with Harold Arlen, she always remembered the unlikelihood of believably passing Betty Grable off as a cook on the Erie Canal.

TODAY I LOVE EVERYBODY

Today I love everybody
Everybody I see;
I hope today is the day I can say
    that
Everybody loves me!

Today I'd give anybody
Anything that I've got;
Today I'd state I think all folks are
    great
Includin' them that are not.

If joy can be contagious
Then catch this wild outrageous
    thing
And get this world to sing:

Today I love everybody,
Everybody I see;
I hope today is the day I can say
    that

Everybody loves everybody
And everybody loves me!

Think the sky is blue
As far as I can see
And should you say the sky is
    gray
It still looks blue to me!
I know the road is wide
I've known it all along
If you decide the road's not wide
Then I'll decide you're wrong

Because

Today, I love everybody
Everybody I see;
I hope today's the day I can say
    that
Everybody loves me!

heights. Yet it ran precisely three more performances than its pre-decessor, closing after an eight-month run.

Dorothy would only do one more libretto in her Broadway career, also the last time she would work simultaneously as co-librettist and lyricist. But before that, she finally got the chance to work on a show with her friend Burton Lane, three years after he withdrew from *By the Beautiful Sea*, when they musicalized her brother Joe and Jerome Chodorov's 1941 stage hit *Junior Miss* for television. Shown as a CBS special on December 20, 1957, it starred Don Ameche heading a family whose lives are complicated by his daughter's vivid imagination. Songs included "Junior Miss," "Have Feet Will Dance," and one of Dorothy's personal favorites, which she requested or sang whenever the occasion permitted, the breezy "I'll Buy It."

Dorothy and Herb picked up a project they'd begun before *By the Beautiful Sea*, but which would not reach the stage until early 1959. Originally announced as *The Works!*, it eventually became the Gwen Verdon vehicle *Redhead*. For Dorothy, it would represent a low point of personal catastrophe and artistic struggle, yielding some of her least revivable work. Ironically, it would win her her first Tony and be her biggest hit since *Annie Get Your Gun*, thirteen years earlier.

It was shortly after *Annie Get Your Gun* opened that brother and sister had had the idea for doing a murder-mystery musical set in a waxworks, like Mme. Tussaud's. The development process was a long and bumpy one, for which Dorothy would write the lyrics. Rodgers and Hammerstein were to produce, but when Dorothy found that the idea wasn't working and they'd need to start again from scratch, Rodgers and Hammerstein withdrew and moved on. Seven years and a number of Fields projects later, the property was optioned by producers Robert Fryer (of *A Tree Grows in Brooklyn* and *By the Beautiful Sea*) and Lawrence Carr. Albert Hague, the German-born, conservatory-trained composer who'd had a hit with *Plain and Fancy*, was hired to do the score, and the show was slated

Renowned Broadway and nightclub singer Mae Barnes in *By the Beautiful Sea*, 1954

THOUGH DEVASTATED BY JEROME KERN'S DEATH,

Dorothy went on to develop successful partnerships with composers like Arthur Schwartz, but she never really got over the profound loss of her mentor and friend. After his death, Kern's wife, Eva, sent Dorothy a melody to which words had never been set. Dorothy's result, almost a decade after his loss, was "April Fooled Me," which remains one of the most poignant in either Dorothy's or Kern's body of work.

The uneven phrase lengths of the lyric reflect Kern's soaring melodic line, his unmistakable trademark. Dorothy was 51 when she wrote this, and her experience and maturity show in the way she handled it. "April" is a subject one might tend to associate more with Oscar Hammerstein. Starting out in the first stanza, it looks like she's heading for that bucolic/poetic territory, especially with the idea that "the drowsy earth would wake up smiling." But unlike her earlier forays into the ardent, like "I Dream Too Much," there is a expert economy and specificity at work. Going on, she turns the thought, and her analogy gives it a sophisticated knowingness; with the very last line, she turns it on us again, introducing the unexpected, and deftly tying up the whole lyric (in a sense, the way she surprises us in her finish of "Remind Me"), ending as Kern's melody began—quietly.

Dorothy's handwritten effort in working out a lyric beginning with "Half a moon is better than no moon." Her entire life, she worked with Black Wing pencils, generally on a legal pad

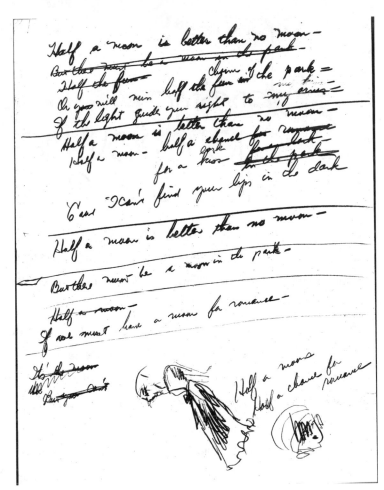

APRIL FOOLED ME

I can remember
So well remember.

Once April fooled me
With an afternoon so gold, so warm, so beguiling,
That I thought the drowsy earth would wake up smiling.
But April fooled me then,
The night was cold.

Once someone fooled me
With a kiss that touched my heart beyond all believing,
But like April, that sweet moment was deceiving.
It was not really spring
Or really love.
You were alike, you two.
Restless April fooled me,
Darling, so did you.

JEROME CHODOROV MET THE FIELDS FAMILY

when, as a young contract writer in 1930s Hollywood, he was teamed with Joe, and together they churned out low-budget movies for Republic Pictures. "When 'I Can't Give You Anything but Love' came out, I was a kid on the beach at Long Beach, and everybody was playing it on their ukeleles," he recalls. "When I first met Joe I was quite overwhelmed by the fact that he was the son of the great Lew Fields. Joe was a sweet man, but very touchy about some things, and he'd get indignant. Moss Hart called him 'Put-Em-Up.'"

Eventually the team gambled on establishing themselves back east, and wrote a string of hit Broadway shows, among them *My Sister Eileen* and the latter's musical incarnation, *Wonderful Town*. Dorothy Fields and Burton Lane later wrote the songs for the musical version of *Junior Miss*, including "I'll Buy It."

I'LL BUY IT

I'll buy it,
Moonight, romance,
Cool quiet
And someone to hold.

I'll grab it,
Marriage, babies,
I'll buy it,
I'm finally sold.

I was a lonely potato,
Completely lost in the stew.

But then no single potato
Is lonely when there are two.

Consequently,

I'll love it.
That wedding ring feeling,
I'll buy it
And pray when I buy it
I'll sell it to you.

A youthful Joe Fields in a publicity
shot for early performing aspirations

for the following season. (Hague would later be remembered for playing the role of the music teacher in the movie and TV show *Fame*.)

But 1958 would turn out to be the worst year of Dorothy's life. While preparing the latest version of the *Redhead* libretto, Herb Fields died of a heart attack, on March 24. Four months later Dorothy also lost her husband, Eli, who died suddenly of a stroke. It was at the same time that her son left home for Amherst College, leaving Dorothy and her teenage daughter alone, for the first time, in an empty house.

Dorothy, whose world had almost instantaneously collapsed on itself, was devastated and reeling from the shock. Her drinking (a problem for some time) got worse, as did her ability to focus on the work at hand, and for the moment, she seemed lost without Herb. Her adored brother had been such an inseparable part of not only her personal, but her professional life all through the decades that even when she regained the order of her world, she never quite got over being without him. (She and Joe had never been as close.) Producers Fryer and Carr, getting nervous about the schedule, called in writers Sidney Sheldon and David Shaw to help her get the book into shape. By that time, the show had been rewritten and reshaped to accommodate, at different times, Celeste Holm, Ethel Merman, and particularly Beatrice Lillie, who disappeared from New York when the contract was to be signed. The creators then auditioned the piece for Gwen Verdon, and as everyone present (including Bob Fosse) sat down and lit up cigarettes, Dorothy, stylishly turned out, as was her custom, related the murder-mystery story, sketched the colorful possibilities and described the characters. Verdon loved the idea, and agreed to do it—on the condition that Fosse, her longtime alter ego and soon-to-be husband, would direct the show as well as choreograph. It would place him at the helm as director for the first time in his career, but his talent and, mostly, the irresistible prospect of Verdon as the show's star made the producers' choice a clear-cut one. The show was promptly renamed *Redhead* in Verdon's honor.

Verdon, who'd come to fame a few years before when she'd stopped the show nightly in *Can-Can* (much to the consternation of the star, Lilo), had once been a protégée and dance assistant of choreographer-Svengali Jack Cole. Through her association with Fosse and the subsequent *Damn Yankees* and *New Girl in Town*, she had rapidly become the most sensational dancing star the musical theatre had ever seen.

In *Redhead*, she played the Edwardian cockney "spinster" Essie Whimple, who works on the wax figures in the London wax museum owned by her aunts, the Simpson sisters. (Mme. Tussaud's had gotten snippy about the use of their establishment's name.) The story involves Essie's visions and a mysterious strangler who's stalking London, and Essie's romantic attraction to American vaudevillian Tom Baxter (played by Richard Kiley). As director, Fosse immediately showed his brilliant theatrical vision, allowing the cartoonish action to be shaped by his dance vocabulary. There was also fun with the waxworks setting and a Mack Sennett-style chase through it to catch the murderer. And of course Fosse used his trademark black bowler hats and canes, which he coupled with dressing the dancers in black leotards, against period, for theatrical effect. The score had a turn-of-the-century music hall flavor, and Dorothy had written a set of deft lyrics, which, if they wouldn't stand among her most pioneering, certainly had charm. Among the songs were "Merely Marvelous," which Verdon sang on finding she'd fallen in love, "The Right Finger of Me Left Hand," "Look Who's in Love," "The Uncle Sam Rag" (a music hall number), "'Erbie Fitch's Twitch" (with its verbal calisthenics), and "She's Not Enough Woman for Me"/"She's Just Enough Woman for Me," two songs that used the same melody and two different lyrics—the first when Tom Baxter is irritable and critical toward Essie, the next when he's been smitten and changed his proverbial tune.

The book was complicated and convoluted. It couldn't have mattered less. Between Verdon, Fosse, and the musical numbers, the package was one of solid theatrical entertainment. *Redhead* arrived in New York from its Philadelphia and Washington tryouts

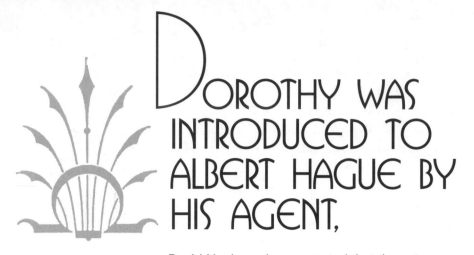

DOROTHY WAS INTRODUCED TO ALBERT HAGUE BY HIS AGENT,

David Hocker, who suggested that the veteran lyricist team with the young German composer, who'd recently had a Broadway success with *Plain and Fancy* (which had introduced Barbara Cook). They collaborated on the waxworks musical that she and Herb had been developing for years, which would eventually open as *Redhead*, in honor of its last in a long line of proposed leading ladies, Gwen Verdon. Verdon's about-to-be husband, Bob Fosse, directed for the first time in his career. Under Fosse's authority (he was some twenty-five years Dorothy's junior), by the time the show opened only three of the Fields-Hague songs remained out of the thirteen they had originally auditioned for him and Verdon.

"It's very difficult to tell somebody you don't like something," Hague says. "So we would play him a song, and he would say, 'No, that's . . .' And Dorothy would say, 'Well you can't just say "no." Why don't you like it?' And he would lean over to her and look her in the face and say, 'It just doesn't entertain me enough.' But he was almost always right. And Dorothy was a consummate professional. So she would be very upset, and later say things like, 'Do you know what that skinny chorus boy said to me yesterday?' And I said, 'That skinny chorus boy happens to be your director,' and she'd say, 'I know' and she would then come up with four new ideas. She was accustomed to having tough people work to work with."

'ERBIE FITCH'S TWITCH

'Erbie Fitch is me name an' I'm
  in rather a pickle
I must say, to me shame, I'm
  fickle.
Ipswich England's me 'ome.
I married something called
  Emma.
One night I chanced to roam
And roamed into a dilemma.

I've a bit of a twitch for a witch I
  met in Ipswich.
But the hitch is the Ipswich witch
  which once I wed.
If I should un-hitch the witch
  which I wed
And switch to the witch which
  gives me the twitch,

The witch which I ditch will pitch
  a rock at me 'ead.

What a petunia!

Tho' I can't lose the itch
The itch for that witch in Ipswich,
The witch which I wed is richer
  than the witch to which I'm led.
Now look, 'Erbie Fitch, you don't
  own a stitch,
Don't switch to the witch which
  gives you a twitch,
Which witch is not rich as the
  witch you wed instead,
Crawl into your niche and take
  Missus Fitch to bed.

REDHEAD

MUSICAL NUMBERS

ACT I

Scene 1: "The Simpson Sisters" . . . . .Singers and Dancers

Scene 2: "The Right Finger of My Left Hand" . . . . .Gwen Verdon

Scene 3: "Just for Once" . . . . .Gwen Verdon, Richard Kiley
and Leonard Stone

Scene 3: "Merely Marvelous" . . . . .Gwen Verdon

Scene 5: "The Uncle Sam Rag" . . . . .Leonard Stone, Singers
and Dancers

Scene 5: "She's Not Enough Woman for Me" . . . . .Richard Kiley,
Leonard Stone

Scene 6: "Behave Yourself" . . . . .Gwen Verdon, Cynthia Latham,
Doris Rich and Richard Kiley

Scene 7: "Look Who's in Love" . . . . .Gwen Verdon and Richard Kiley

Scene 8: "My Girl Is Just Enough Woman for Me" . . . . .Richard Kiley and Passersby

Scene 9: "Essie's Vision" . . . . .Gwen Verdon
and Her Dream People

Scene 10: "Two Faces in the Dark" . . . . .Gwen Verdon, Bob Dixon,
Singers and Dancers

ACT II

Scene 1: "I'm Back in Circulation" . . . . .Richard Kiley

Scene 3: "We Loves Ya, Jimey" . . . . .Gwen Verdon, Joy Nichols,
Pat Ferrier and Clientele
of the Green Dragon

Scene 4: "Pick-Pocket Tango" . . . . .Gwen Verdon and Buzz Miller

Scene 5: "Look Who's in Love" (Reprise) . . . . .Richard Kiley

Scene 6: "I'll Try" . . . . .Gwen Verdon and Richard Kiley

Scene 6: Finale . . . . .Gwen Verdon, Richard Kiley
and Company

Left: Gwen Verdon in the role previously written for Bea Lillie. *Redhead*, 1958

to open at the 46th Street Theatre on February 5, 1959, and was the hit of the season. The critics gave it virtually unanimous raves, particularly for Gwen Verdon, over whom they were positively giddy. "Choreographer Bob Fosse keeps thinking up fetching postures, parades, chases, and tailspins for her to dive unblinkingly into," wrote Walter Kerr in the *Herald Tribune*, "and she dives—well, magnificently." Richard Watts, Jr., wrote in the *Post*, "You would have to go back to memories of Gertrude Lawrence to find a kinship in charm, skill and authentic glamour. . . ." John Chapman summed up in the *Daily News*, "Now we have four really tip-top musicals in town—*My Fair Lady, West Side Story, The Music Man*, and *Redhead*. And the new one has something that the other three haven't got: namely, Gwen Verdon."

At the Tony Awards ceremony, the *Redhead* contingent practically had to take their honors home in a shopping cart. It won nine awards, including Best Musical, beating out *Flower Drum Song, Goldilocks*, and *Whoop-Up*. Albert Hague won as Best Composer; Bob Fosse won for the choreography; Fryer and Carr collected as producers; Gwen Verdon and Richard Kiley both won, as did supporting actor Leonard Stone, who tied with Russell Nype for *Goldilocks*; Rouben Ter-Arutunian took home the award for Costume Design. Dorothy collected not only her own Tony for the libretto, but Herb's as well. What had begun in the most traumatic circumstances had ended up covered in glory. *Redhead* would run a healthy 455 performances, and Dorothy would finish out the 1950s with one of the biggest hits of her career.

1960–1974

FOR THE FIRST TIME in Dorothy's career, there was a gap of seven years until the opening of her next show. Eli's and Herb's deaths had left her with both personal and professional grief, and she needed time to readjust. Not that she wouldn't have welcomed a good job if it had come her way, something in which to immerse herself, just as she'd done steadily all her life. But nothing fell into her lap, and her lack of a steady collaborator didn't make it any easier in a changing Broadway landscape, where projects were more often initiated with the creative side, rather than the more old-fashioned practice of producers simply signing this composer or that lyricist for a job. She hadn't developed any kind of a relationship with Albert Hague after *Redhead*; Arthur Schwartz was living in London.

Besides, Broadway was now largely in the hands of a new generation. Nineteen-sixty brought the death of her old friend and emotional link to Jerome Kern Oscar Hammerstein, who succumbed to cancer some months after the opening of *The Sound of Music*, marking the formal end of the Rodgers and Hammerstein era. That year, the runaway hit was the farthest thing from a Rodgers and Hammerstein show—the catchy, satirical, youth-oriented *Bye Bye Birdie*, with a score by young turks Charles Strouse and Lee Adams that was much closer in style to the old Abbott college musicals. The late '50s and early '60s saw a crop of young talents coming into their own and reshaping the musical theatre once again: Jerry Bock and Sheldon Harnick, who'd written *Fiorello!* and *She Loves Me* and were about to write *Fiddler on the Roof*; Jerry Herman, with *Hello, Dolly!* and *Mame*; John Kander and Fred Ebb, with *Flora, the Red Menace* and *Cabaret*; Cy Coleman and Carolyn Leigh with *Wildcat* and *Little Me*; Harvey Schmidt and Tom Jones, with *The Fantasticks* and *I Do! I Do!*; and Stephen Sondheim, who had recently begun his meteoric career with *West Side Story*, *Gypsy*, and *A Funny*

Thing Happened on the Way to the Forum. The stylistic changes the
musical theatre was undergoing were largely shaped by the choreo-
graphers-turned-directors that included Jerome Robbins, Bob
Fosse, and Gower Champion, who saw
the world through stylized, movement-
driven shorthand.

Dorothy, now in her late fifties,
was not alone in her feelings that her
profession had somehow passed her
by. Her contemporaries who had
not retired were experiencing the
same frustrations of forced inactivity or projects that met with little
enthusiasm: Alan Jay Lerner, Yip
Harburg, Harold Arlen, Burton Lane, and
even Richard Rodgers, who had only one moderately
successful show (*No Strings*) after Hammerstein's death. (Dorothy,
in fact, was heard to note that her girlhood beau never requested
her services as lyricist, though Rodgers went on to collaborate with
the young Stephen Sondheim, Martin Charnin, and Sheldon
Harnick.)

Moving again, from the Park Avenue apartment to Central Park
West and 81st Street, she settled into a spacious abode overlooking
the park at number 211—also known as the Beresford—filling the
place with English antiques, lots of chintz and flowers, and her
teapot collection. She also sold the house in Brewster that had been
for so long the center of her family life, trading it for a country place
on the eastern shore of Long Island, in Bridgehampton.

If sometimes her feelings of bitterness and frustration at being
shortchanged on recognition would bubble out, it was only private-
ly, among family, and it was usually after a couple of drinks. Her
friends, who may have sensed a vague unhappiness about her in her
later years, were not usually regaled with any melancholy gripes.
Though her own drinking problem only worsened with time, her
warmth, wit, and generosity were held in such esteem that her
friends went out of their way to protect her. One longtime friend
speculated that all the cushioning ultimately just allowed her to
avoid facing reality: "Everybody loved Dorothy—you didn't want to
hurt her."

Nevertheless, in the fallow years of the early '60s, Dorothy, chicly maintained as ever, continued an active theatregoing and social life, transferring her occasional partygiving to the new apartment, and she worked hard for her charities. There was an occasional man in her life, particularly, in her later years, a constant companion named Earl Earle.

But Dorothy was about to have a professional rebirth, which began when talented young composer Cy Coleman approached her, in a rather gutsy move, to inquire of the veteran some twenty-five years his senior about the possibility of their working together. Dorothy was intrigued. Coleman had written *Wildcat* several years earlier as a vehicle for Lucille Ball. Directed and choreographed by Michael Kidd, with a book by N. Richard Naish (*The Rainmaker*), it had been a general disappointment and had failed, but it had a bright score that included the immense song hit "Hey, Look Me Over." The satire *Little Me*, which was based on Patrick (*Auntie Mame*) Dennis's novel in the form of a mock memoir, had opened two years later and starred Sid Caesar, with a book by Neil Simon. Coleman had been working with Carolyn Leigh, a talented woman lyricist who was part of Dorothy's legacy (and with whom he'd written pop hits like "Witchcraft"), and the show had been codirected and choreographed by Bob Fosse.

So when in 1965 Fosse moved ahead on a musical based on the Federico Fellini film *Nights of Cabiria* as another vehicle for Gwen Verdon (now Mrs. Fosse and mother of their infant daughter), both Dorothy and Coleman were signed for the project, again produced by Robert Fryer and Lawrence Carr. Originally, Fosse had conceived *Sweet Charity* as two one-acts, one each written by Elaine May and himself, but it was soon evident that what he had in his draft of the script was a full-length show. The original contract bears Fosse's name as the author of the book, but realizing he needed help, he called on his friend Neil Simon to work it through, and Fosse eventually relinquished authorship.

Simon was currently the most commercially successful playwright on Broadway, with *Barefoot in the Park* and *The Odd Couple*

After a Number of Years of Frustrating

professional inactivity Dorothy met Cy Coleman one night at a party at Sheldon Harnick's house. The composer of *Wildcat* and *Little Me* had recently ended his stormy collaboration with lyricist Carolyn Leigh. "I asked Dorothy if she'd ever consider collaborating," he says. "I told her, 'I'd like to write a song or two with you.' She said, 'Thank God somebody asked.' I was surprised. Here was this legendary figure waiting around to be asked."

Their working relationship was smoother than his with Leigh, partly because Coleman deferred to Dorothy's age. The biggest problem was Dorothy's need to work in the morning, while Coleman, a bon vivant who still liked to perform in clubs, was on a different schedule. "But we also liked to do certain portions of the work on our own," he says, "and then show each other what we'd done later. That worked out well because she had those mornings quiet and to herself, free of any possible interruptions from me."

Working with her team of thirty-something collaborators, the sixty-year-old Dorothy was doing lyrics for her first musical set in the current day in over twenty-five years of costume dramas. Interestingly, her songs like "Big Spender" and "If My Friends Could See Me Now" are vintage slangy, street-smart 1920s Dorothy Fields, with the maturity and expertise of the Broadway veteran.

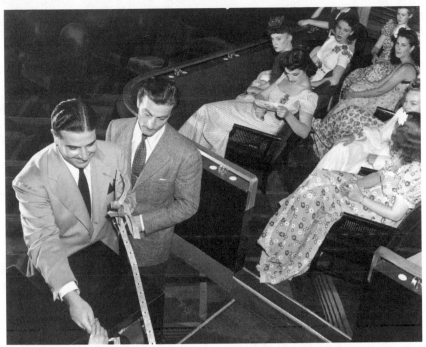

A real Broadway dance hall, like the one that provides the setting for *Sweet Charity*. At right, the hostesses, or "taxi dancers," wait for their customers.

BIG SPENDER

The minute you walked in the
   joint,
I could see you were a man of
   distinction,
A real big spender,
Good looking, so refined.
Say, wouldn't you like to know
   what's going on in my mind?
So let me get right to the point,
I don't pop my cork for every
   guy I see.
Hey! Big Spender, spend a little
   time with me.

Wouldn't you like to have fun,
   fun, fun?
Hows about a few laughs,
   laughs?

I can show you a good time,
Let me show you a good time.

The minute you walked in the
   joint,
I could see you were a man of
   distinction,
A real big spender,
Good looking, so refined.
Say, wouldn't you like to know
   what's going on in my mind?
So let me get right to the point
I don't pop my cork for every
   guy I see
Hey! Big Spender,
Hey! Big Spender,
Spend a little time with me.

running. He fashioned the script for *Sweet Charity* as an episodic series of sketches in the life of Charity Hope Valentine, a dance-hall hostess (or "taxi dancer") at the sleazy Fan-Dango Ballroom. (As a concession to American morality, they'd changed Charity's profession from the world's oldest, as it had been in the Fellini version with Giulietta Masina.) The story chronicles the Chaplinesque, lovable victim on the road to self-realization through a series of encounters with men who treat her abominably, all because of her generous "big, fat heart." It is subtitled "The Story of a Girl Who Wanted to Be Loved."

The feel of *Sweet Charity* was very contemporary, with a texture that mixed old-fashioned Broadway values, the jazzy, burlesquey ambiance of the seamy ballroom life with its varying dance rhythms, and a wry nod to the mid-'60s swingers' scene. (It was the first time an electrified keyboard, a "Rocksachord," was used in a Broadway orchestra—utilized during numbers like the typical Fosse set piece "Rich Man's Frug.")

Stylistically, this was the show where Fosse became "Fosse" not only in the choreography but in the overall look and presentation of the show—his trademark combination of a skewed, minimalist take and plain showmanship. This was demonstrated in everything from the sexually charged come-ons of the Fan-Dango Girls (led by Helen Gallagher and Thelma Oliver) to the humorous vulnerability of the not-so-innocent innocent who begins and ends the fable being pushed into Central Park Lake.

Coleman's score perfectly captured the many rhythms of the story (more than just a theatre composer, he'd had success playing jazz piano with a combo in clubs, and knew well the life of a man about town). Like the other principals on the creative team—Fosse, Verdon, and Simon—he was still in his thirties. Dorothy had just turned sixty.

Perhaps it was the youth of her collaborators or the very contemporary subject (the first since 1939 and *Stars in Your Eyes*) that galvanized Dorothy's energy and caused her to turn out the score for which she will always be remembered. The lyrics she wrote with

Coleman for *Sweet Charity* synthesized her mature expertise with the integral, character-revealing theatre lyrics and rhythmic dialogue that she'd striven for all her career. Even more than in *A Tree Grows in Brooklyn*, there is a sharpness and clarity to *Sweet Charity*'s succession of lyrics that define the essence of theatre-lyricist Fields. If any lyricist of her generation was right for this project, it was Dorothy Fields, because the hallmark of her style had always been her uncanny ear for the colloquial, which in real time perpetually changes from moment to moment. As Dorothy had gotten older, she hadn't become mired in a "well in my day . . ." or "they don't write songs like that anymore . . ." sensibility like so many others. As proper and ladylike as she presented herself to the world, her ear and mind were constantly open to the changes that music, speech, and culture were undergoing. The only evidence of her years that shows up in the *Sweet Charity* work is her seasoned ability and confidence.

Besides being contemporary in setting, *Sweet Charity* was a child of a trend in the musical theatre that had been visible in *West Side Story* and recently in *Gypsy*: although it had a central humanity, it was dark. It had an edge, an irony, a look that was always showmanlike but not always pretty. For Dorothy and her own particular arsenal, capturing the street-smart talk and the largely uneducated, tough-but-lovable oddballs who populated the Fan-Dango and vicinities was like being locked in a candy store. What came out was a slangy lingo and perceptiveness that took her, in feel, back to her roots—the early songs with Jimmy McHugh like "I Can't Give You Anything But Love" and "On the Sunny Side of the Street."

The very first song in *Sweet Charity*, in which, by the Central Park lake, Charity showers a stonily indifferent boyfriend with compliments, is quintessential Fields, updated.

SWEET CHARITY

SYNOPSIS OF SCENES
AND MUSICAL NUMBERS

ACT I

PROLOGUE—CHARITY'S WISH

SCENE 1. THE PARK

"You Should See Yourself" . . . . .Gwen Verdon, Michael Davis

"The Rescue" . . . . .Gwen Verdon and the Passsers-by

SCENE 2. HOSTESS ROOM

SCENE 3. FAN-DANGO BALLROOM

"Big Spender" . . . . .Helen Gallagher and Thelma Oliver
and the Fan-Dango Girls

"Charity's Soliloquy" . . . . .Gwen Verdon

SCENE 4. NEW YORK STREET

SCENE 5. POMPEII CLUB

"Rich Man's Frug" . . . . .Barbara Sharma, Eddie Gasper
and John Sharpe—The Patrons

SCENE 6. VITTORIO VIDAL'S APARTMENT

"If My Friends Could See Me Now" . . . . .Gwen Verdon

"Too Many Tomorrows" . . . . .James Luisi

SCENE 6A. VITTORIO VIDAL'S APARTMENT (A NEW DAY)

SCENE 7. HOSTESS ROOM

"There's Gotta Be Something Better Than This" . . . . . . .Gwen Verdon,
Helen Gallagher,
Thelma Oliver

SCENE 8. YMHA—ELEVATOR

"I'm the Bravest Individual" . . . . .Gwen Verdon, John McMartin

ACT II

GWEN VERDON, NEEDING A FIRSTHAND GLANCE

into the life of a taxi dancer, actually went to work in a Broadway dance palace for awhile to absorb the atmosphere. Her price? In 1965 her customers were paying $6.50 an hour, plus an additional $1.50 admission.

IF MY FRIENDS COULD SEE ME NOW

If they could see me now, that
   little gang of mine,
I'm eating fancy chow and drinking fancy wine.
I'd like those stumblebums to
   see for a fact
The kind of top drawer, first rate
   chums I attract.

All I can say is "Wowee! Looka
   where I am.
Tonight I landed, pow! Right in a
   pot of jam."
What a setup! Holy cow!
They'd never believe it,
If my friends could see me now!

If they could see me now, my
   little dusty group,
Traipsin' 'round this million dollar
   chicken coop.
I'd hear those thrift shop cats
   say: "Brother, get her!
Draped on a bedspread made
   from three kinds of fur."

All I can say is "Wow! Wait till the
   riff and raff
See just exactly how he signed
   this autograph."
What a buildup! Holy cow!
They'd never believe it,
If my friends could see me now!

If they could see me now
Alone with Mister V.
Who's waitin' on me like he was
   a Maitre d'.
I hear my buddies saying "Crazy,
   what gives?
Tonight she's living like the other
   half lives."

To think the highest brow, which
   I must say is he,
Should pick the lowest brow,
   which there's no doubt is me.
What a stepup! Holy cow!
They'd never believe it,
If my friends could see me now!

Gwen Verdon, in her trademark role of "a girl who wanted to be loved." *Sweet Charity*, 1966. "If My Friends Could See Me Now"

Man! Man, oh man,
You should see yourself, like tonight,
You're a hundred watt e-lec-a-tric light.
You're a blockbuster, buster, you got class
And when you make a pass, man,
It's a pass.

Mad, Jack, you're mad. Mmm mmm!
How those corny jokes turn me on!
And I laugh till I'm "ga-ga-ga-ga-gone!"
When you switch to a se-duc-a-tive mood
I'm not stuck on you lover,
I am glued.

The lyric immediately establishes the character's personality—at once her background, and the cartwheels she perpetually turns to try and please. (He promptly takes her bag and pushes her in.) Additionally, Dorothy signals that in this score she has moved beyond "safe," standard structural devices to reach further, particularly in the way she handles Charity's monologizing throughout the show, blurring the line between song and rhythmic speech.

Dorothy and Coleman do the same for the girls of the Fan-Dango and the *noir* song "Big Spender" with its stripper-aura beat and the seductive lyrics that taunt and lie ("I could tell you were a man of distinction"), in the girls' attempt to improve business, to the losers who frequent the joint. In "Charity's Soliloquy" she recounts her affair with the last heel, whom she met showing him the way to Bloomingdale's, then paid for his purchases and his taxicab and allowed him to move in with her when he was kicked out of his furnished room; then finding herself in love, she found him to be mainly concerned about her getting "a better-paying job." Heartbroken, she vows to change her ways.

Along with "Big Spender," the show's enormous popular hit (and showstopper) was "If My Friends Could See Me Now," which Charity sings from the apartment of an Italian movie star, not believing the heights to which she's risen, and exuberantly proclaiming (with the requisite Fosse hat and cane):

I'd hear those thrift shop cats say:
"Brother, get her!
Draped on a bedspread made from
three kinds of fur."

Other songs were "There's Gotta Be Something Better than This," in which Charity and her two friends resolve to get out of the Fan-Dango life; "I'm the Bravest Individual," in which Charity calms Oscar, a claustrophobic accountant (played by John McMartin) while trapped in an elevator at the 92nd Street Y on the way to a lecture on "Free Thought in Active Society"; a neogospel/rock number in a hippie church called "The Rhythm of Life"; the self-questioning "Where Am I Going?"; "I'm a Brass Band," in which Charity revels in the discovery that someone loves her; and the ensemble sendoff given her by her Fan-Dango friends, Coleman's infectious polka "I Love to Cry at Weddings."

In Coleman, Dorothy had found a perfect collaborator. His energy sharpened her contemporary focus, and her experience lent their work mastery and polish. In contrast to her relationships with her previous major collaborators McHugh and Kern, for the first time Dorothy was the veteran of the pair. Dorothy, who always worked fast once she had the idea for a lyric, generally sat and wrote with a yellow legal pad and Black Wing pencil at a table in her apartment as she always had. But with Coleman, she would often join him by the piano, and they'd work things out almost simultaneously.

They finished "I Love to Cry at Weddings" on November 9, 1965, the evening the Big Blackout hit New York City, and they rushed over to where Fosse was rehearsing a dance number and sang it to him; then they were so pleased, they sang it out the window to the darkened city. One of Dorothy's favorite songs, "Pink Taffeta Sample Size 10," was cut when the show lost a scene, and

IN THE LINEAGE OF WOMEN LYRICISTS/ COMPOSERS

of the American songbook and musical theatre, Betty Comden was the natural successor to Dorothy Fields. A generation after Fields, she appeared in the mid-1940s with the hit *On the Town* (after Dorothy had been a star for almost twenty years), and was herself a lone female island until joined by others like Carolyn Leigh (*Little Me*) and Mary Rodgers (*Once Upon a Mattress*) in the 1950s, paving the way for the slew of women who then steadily entered the forefront of the songwriting fields of both musical theatre and pop music—from Gretchen Cryer (*I'm Getting My Act Together and Taking It on the Road*) and Carol Hall (*Best Little Whorehouse in Texas*) to Carole King, Joni Mitchell, and Carly Simon. Interestingly, Comden is one of the professionals who does not believe that Dorothy Fields lyrics particularly show themselves to be written by a woman.

"I don't think there is a female voice there," she says, "I think those songs could have been written by either a man or a woman."

Shirley MacLaine in the film version of *Sweet Charity*

I LOVE TO CRY AT WEDDINGS

It's tough for a loudmouth mug
  like me
Who all the time bellows like a
  bull,
To make with the words about
  the Mrs.-to-be
When what you think is an empty
  heart is full.
Tomorrow when you say, "I do,"
  I'll die.
I'm almost too ashamed to tell
  you why

I love to cry at weddings,
How I love to cry at weddings,
I walk into a chapel and get hap-
  pily hysterical,

The ushers and attendants,
The family dependents,

I see them and I start to sniff,
Have you an extra handkerchief?

And all through the service
While the bride and groom look
  nervous
Tears of joy are streaming down
  my face.
I love to cry at weddings, any-
  body's wedding
Anytime! Anywhere, anyplace.

And all through the service
While the bride and groom look
  nervous
I drink champagne and sing
  "Sweet Adeline."
I love to cry at weddings, any-
  body's wedding
Just as long as it's not mine!

later became a favorite of Sylvia Syms in cabaret. At the tryout in Detroit, Fosse insisted that one of two slow songs needed to come out, and gave the authors a choice of "Where Am I Going?" or "Poor Everybody Else." They decided "Where Am I Going?" did more for the story, and "Poor Everybody Else" would eventually be recycled for their next show, *Seesaw*. "The Rhythm of Life" was written (on a Saturday afternoon and part of Sunday) in Detroit for the church-in-a-garage scene, replacing a song called "Gimme a Raincheck," which everybody agreed wasn't working (Dorothy would refer to it bluntly as "a stinker"). When the tryout moved to Philadelphia and another song was needed, Dorothy, who was working with Coleman at the Warwick Hotel, got the first line in her head, "I'm a brass band, I'm a harpsichord." They called Fosse in his room at the same hotel to run it by him, he said "Do it," and they wrote it in short order.

Fosse was spooked because his long streak of unstoppable success had ended with two failures; the last was the rather spectacular failure of Frank Loesser's *Pleasures and Palaces* (1965), which had closed out of town in none other than Detroit. But from Charity's opening, greeted by the *Detroit Free Press* headline "Goodbye Dolly. Hello Charity. Hail Gwen!," *Sweet Charity* seemed destined to be an overwhelming hit. It played four standing-room-only weeks, and then moved on to Philadelphia, where it had a $35,000 advance for its two weeks there. Declared the *Evening Bulletin*, "*Sweet Charity* Arrives—Bless It!"

The show's arrival in New York also marked the reopening of the 1,720-seat Palace Theatre, which had just been refurbished and reclaimed as a legit house, having fallen on dilapidated times after it was the jewel of the Orpheum vaudeville circuit early in the century. *Sweet Charity* moved in to open on January 29, 1966, with a one-million-dollar advance. Opening-night tickets were fifteen dollars, but there wasn't a seat to be had until July. The first-night audience was on its feet thundering the house down as Verdon stopped the show with practically every number.

Surprisingly, the New York critics were much less enchanted by the show than their out-of-town colleagues. The reviews, however, were solid enough. Some, like John Chapman of the *Daily News*, liked it: he wrote: "It can't miss," touting Dorothy Fields's "intelligently wrought" lyrics and Bob Fosse's dances "among the best to be seen in the theatre."

Gwen Verdon got her customary adulation, though with less giddy abandon, it seemed, than for *Redhead*, which had been her last appearance on Broadway. Even the favorable reviews protested what they felt was a pall cast by the bittersweet ending in which Charity is abandoned once more, by (or in) the lake.

It was Stanley Kauffmann of the *Times* who criticized the show most vehemently, writing (with shades of the *Annie Get Your Gun* reviews twenty years earlier) of Coleman's music that there were "no tunes that can be remembered," and calling the lyrics "no more than servicable." He went on to say about Simon's book and Fosse's work that it was "not 'The story of a girl who wanted to be loved,'" but "the story of a *show* that wants to be loved."

Happily, audiences didn't see it that way and came in droves, making it not only one of the biggest hits of the season (it ran 608 performances before touring and had a London production), but ultimately one of the most enduring works of the American musical theatre. (There would also be a major Broadway revival in 1985, with Debbie Allen.)

The continuing success of *Sweet Charity* was driven in part by the breakout hits "Big Spender" and "If My Friends Could See Me Now," and by the fact that "Where Am I Going?" was promptly recorded by Barbra Streisand. The songs were everywhere in the national consciousness—including radio and television. By the mid '60s, this was already rare for a song coming out of Broadway, which, before the "integrated" musical and the arrival of rock and roll, had been the pop world's primary source.

For Dorothy, it meant not only personal and financial success, but rejuvenation. Unlike virtually any composer or lyricist of her generation, she was, in her sixties, a viable commodity with a

DOROTHY EVENTUALLY GOT INTO THE HABIT

of reading out loud to her children the lyrics she had finished that morning. Her daughter, Eliza, remembers, "We'd say, 'That's great.' I can only remember one song that she read to me that I just hated. It was 'Pink Taffeta Sample Size 10.' And I said, 'That's so sappy, I just hate it, it's corny.' And she really got ticked. She got so upset, I realized that basically she wanted reassurance— not a sixteen-year-old's critique of her lyrics. I don't know . . . She asked me . . . .

"But most of her lyrics were so brilliant and funny, we could definitely appreciate them. I remember her reading me "Erbie Fitch' from *Redhead*. I thought it was hilarious. She had a wonderful way with words when she spoke, too. She was very interested in words. She never went to college, and she was the kind of person that if she didn't know a word, she would go look it up. And if we didn't know a word and we asked her, she'd say, 'Go look it up.'"

"Rich Man's Frug," *Sweet Charity*, 1966. Sixty-year-old Dorothy never lagged behind the times.

PINK TAFFETA SAMPLE SIZE 10

When I was a kid, Pop went on
   the road,
Winter and Summer
He was a traveling salesman,
What the trade called a drummer.

He worked for a firm called
   Juvenile Frocks
And once and so often he'd
   bring home a box
That was the box I'd fall on,
If my hands were clean Pop let
   me try them all on.

Number five-fifty-three: the juvenile frock for me
I loved five-fifty-three.

It was copied from an import, it
   was real Parisienne
First I'd model it for Ma,
Than I'd hand it back to Pa
The pink taffeta sample, size ten.

It had twenty-seven buttons,
Which were sewed on very
   straight
And the skirt spread like a fan
And besides it fit me better than
   the blue organdy sample, size
   eight

Then my dream went in the suit-
   case
Papa had to catch a train
And it could never be mine,
He would sell it off the line in
   Scranton, Pennsylvania

Then on my eleventh birthday
Pop was way out in Cheyenne
That's the birthday I love most
'Cause what came by parcel
   post?
A pink taffeta sample, size ten

Never thought I'd own a pink
   taffeta sample, size ten.

TRAUMATIZED BY THE DEATHS IN THE SAME YEAR

of her husband, Eli, and brother Herb, Dorothy struggled with her depression and the need to attend to her children, who were not yet grown—Eliza, in high school, and David, who would return to the Park Avenue apartment on his breaks from Amherst College.

"When I came home I lived like a real slob," David recalls. "I just took over the couch in my mother's study, stayed out late, slept late, went around the house and played the piano when I wanted to, listened to a lot of records—probably was a real pain in the ass. She allowed me to do this. I mean there were times she got really mad at what a slob I was. But basically, she understood that maybe there was some creative talent that I had, and this was the time I was really motivated to pursue it. So she was going to be supportive of this the best way she could. And it was very difficult times for her."

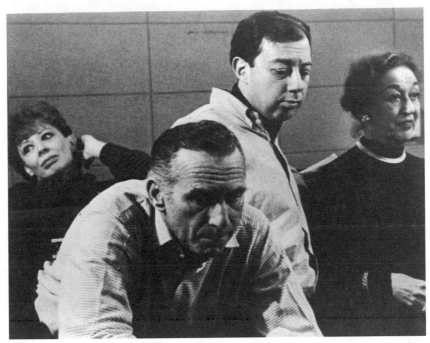

Rehearsal for Columbia Records' recording of *Charity* original cast album, 1966. L to r: Gwen Verdon, Columbia Records chief Goddard Lieberson, Cy Coleman, and Dorothy

WHERE AM I GOING?

Where am I going, and what will I find?
What's in this grab bag that I call my mind?
What am I doing alone on the shelf?
Ain't it a shame, but no one's to blame but myself.
Which way is clear
When you've lost your way year after year?

Do I keep falling in love for just the kick of it?
Staggering through the thin and thick of it,
Hating each old and tired trick of it,
Know what I am, I'm good and sick of it!
Where am I going?
Why do I care?
Run to the Bronx, or Washington Square,
No matter where I run, I meet myself there.

Looking inside me, what do I see?
Anger and hope and doubt,
What am I all about?
And where am I going?
You tell me!

collaborator at the forefront of the business. But though she and Coleman had every intention of continuing their partnership and began working on a couple of projects, it would be another seven years before they'd have their next show on Broadway—and even then, *Seesaw* almost didn't make it.

In 1965–66 *Sweet Charity* had cost some $200,000+ to produce. In 1973 *Seesaw* was budgeted at $750,000 and ended up costing well over a million. Economics had rapidly become the dominating factor in the Broadway theatre, with veteran producers reeling from the circumstances. The "nice little show" that could have a modest run and make back its investment had become a thing of the past. Any project was a major undertaking that could no longer be financed out of pocket or with a small group of loyal angels. Rodgers and Hammerstein used to write a new show every other year, and in alternate years produce a musical or straight play, like *Annie Get Your Gun* or *Happy Birthday* with Helen Hayes. That kind of timetable now approached fantasyland for both creators and producers.

Complicating things further, the watershed year of 1968 brought the arrival of *Hair*, which was followed in 1971 by *Godspell* and *Jesus Christ Superstar*, all with mammoth runs. The rock musical was sounding the death knell for the traditional musical theatre. Original, nonrock shows would continue to be produced into the '70s and beyond, but only a tiny fraction of what there had been up to the late '60s. Cy Coleman, at the beginning of his prime and contemporary, was still steeped in the Broadway and jazz traditions. While he, along with others like Kander and Ebb and most dramatically Stephen Sondheim, would continue to get his work produced, there would never again be a time in the musical theatre when getting a show on wouldn't be a high-stakes, mine-laden ordeal.

In the years following *Sweet Charity*, Dorothy and Coleman did a song called "Keep It in the Family" for a straight play by the same title, which closed on Broadway after five performances; she did a song with Quincy Jones called "Where There Is

Love, There is Hope," and one called "Five O'Clock Sky" with her son, David Lahm. She was slated at one point to work on the ill-fated musical *The Happy Time*, but it was eventually done by Kander and Ebb; she began work on a show called *The Coffee Lovers* and a musical version of the Charles Boyer and Olivia De Havilland movie *Hold Back the Dawn* (again, an attempt to use unpublished Jerome Kern music). Most notably, in 1970 she and Coleman wrote an entire show called *Eleanor*, with a book by Jerome Coopersmith, about the young Eleanor Roosevelt and her romance with Franklin. Announced by producer Alexander H. Cohen for the 1970–71 season, it was to be directed by Morton (*The Music Man*) Da Costa and slated to go into rehearsals by December or January, but the project didn't come together as hoped and it was never produced. Nor did the Fields-Coleman team realize plans for a musical stage adaption of *Mr. Smith Goes to Washington*, also announced. (It was also announced, following *Sweet Charity*, that the duo would supply songs for the Julie Andrews film vehicle *Thoroughly Modern Millie*. The job ultimately went to Sammy Cahn and James Van Heusen.)

By 1972, however, they had begun work on *Seesaw*. Originally to be called *Gittel*, *Seesaw* was the musical version of William Gibson's two-character play about Gittel Mosca, a flaky, Jewish bohemian dancer who falls for Jerry Ryan, a straightlaced midwestern lawyer, and about their relationship that was destined not to be. The play, which opened on Broadway in 1958 with Henry Fonda and (in her debut) Anne Bancroft, was a big hit that ran almost two years at the Booth and made Anne Bancroft a star. Subsequently, it had been filmed with Robert Mitchum and Shirley MacLaine.

Coleman has said that the backstage story of *Seesaw* is like a 1940s MGM musical. It was more harrowing. Produced by Lawrence Kasha and Joseph Kipness, *Seesaw* was to be directed by Ed Sherin, who had been acclaimed for his direction of *The Great White Hope*. He had never directed a musical before. The book was by Michael Stewart, one of the foremost librettists of the era, with successes including *Bye Bye Birdie*, *Carnival*, and most notably

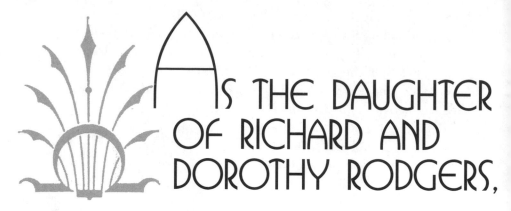

As the daughter of Richard and Dorothy Rodgers,

Mary Rodgers grew up knowing Dorothy Fields as a lifelong friend of both her parents. When she herself began composing for the theatre and had a hit with *Once Upon a Mattress*, which made Carol Burnett a star in 1959, she was suddenly regarded by her parents' friend (who had not yet found Cy Coleman) with new eyes.

"After I'd written *Once Upon a Mattress*," Rodgers says, "she very flatteringly spoke to me about maybe working with her at some point. But the awful thing is I remember thinking, 'I'm not sure I could work with another woman, no matter how great she is, I would need to have a male boss there . . . .' I must have been very young, because I was used to being pushed around by the lyric writers I'd been working with, like Marshall Barer. And so I never followed up on it, which was pretty stupid, when you consider the fact that she was one of the finest lyric writers, ever. I don't remember whether I was in between having children, because it seems like an awfully dumb thing not to have picked up on. I can't think of anybody else that wouldn't have been on the phone the next morning."

Gwen Verdon, Helen Gallagher, and Thelma Oliver, "There's Gotta Be Something Better Than This"

I'M A BRASS BAND

Somebody loves me, my heart is beating so fast.
All kinds of music is pouring out of me,
Somebody loves me at last!

Now,

I'm a brass band, I'm a harpsichord;
I'm a clarinet.
I'm the Philadelphia Orchestra,
I'm the Modern Jazz Quartet.

I'm the band from Macy's big parade.
A wild Count Basie blast.
I'm the bells of St. Peter's in Rome.
I'm tissue paper on a comb.
And all kinds of music is pouring out of me
'Cause somebody loves me at last!

Hello, Dolly! Dorothy and Cy wrote their score over seven months, and *Seesaw* went into rehearsals on November 20, 1972, starring Lainie Kazan as Gittel and Ken Howard as Jerry, along with a cast of singers and dancers. Rehearsals didn't go well. Kazan had trouble learning her lines, and Sherin tried to help, but they fought constantly about interpretation. Meanwhile, the rest of the show wasn't coming together, either technically or in terms of integrating the book with the score. An pall of anxiety settled over the project, which only worsened when an executive from Columbia Records (an investor with the rights to record the show) dropped in unannounced at rehearsal one day and was dismayed at the few numbers he saw along with a fight between Kazan and Sherin; the next day Columbia withdrew its backing.

When, in chaos, the show opened its Detroit tryout, everyone had the flu, and Act One had twenty-three scenes. The local press acknowledged the dancing and music, but was unsympathetic to the other problems, chief among which seemed to be that Lainie Kazan was miscast and nobody believed the character was a dancer (she'd promised to lose forty pounds when she signed, offering to put it in her contract), and she still didn't know all of her part. The producers and creative team decided she must be fired; they enticed Michele Lee (who'd already had suceess on the stage and screen with *How to Succeed in Business Without Really Trying*) to come to Detroit and take over. Then they talked an initially unwilling Michael Bennett (pre–*Chorus Line*) to step in as "artistic director," and he finally agreed under the condition that he be able to start from scratch with a new cast, new sets, new orchestrations, new costumes, and complete artistic control. All agreed, Sherin bowed out, and Bennett fired Kazan, who was furious. (Because the gentlemanly producers had neglected to put the weight clause in her contract, they had to continue paying her $3,000 a week for the run of the play—an obligation divided up and taken on by Stewart, Kasha, Coleman, and Dorothy, since the show soon ran out of money.)

In Detroit, Bennett, the twenty-nine-year-old *wunderkind* who'd choreographed *Follies* (1971), *Company* (1970), and *Coco* (1969), remade the show, fired chorus members to bring in dancers he knew he could work with, and called in the unknown Tommy Tune to help him choreograph and to perform a supporting role. It was late January, and *Seesaw* was scheduled to open on Broadway on March 3.

Bennett had also insisted, in line with his revised conception, that Dorothy and Coleman scrap about half their score and start again. Along with everyone else, both composer and lyricist had the flu, and as Dorothy described it, they "took a box of Kleenex apiece, propped them on the piano, and coughed into each other's faces and wrote three new songs in one week." They would finish with a total of six, with new orchestrations for everything.

Bennett's assistant, Bob Avian, rechoreographed some numbers while the show's original choreographer, Grover Dale, stayed on to help with others. In fact, with Bennett's brilliance and the massive reworking, the company was in a state of organized turmoil, but everybody had worked so hard already that they pulled together in an almost unheard of manner. Stewart's book was still long and problematic, and everybody was rewriting it—Dorothy, Coleman, Bennett, the actors. Neil Simon was called in to cut. Stewart bowed out during previews, taking his name off the show, and Bennett took over credit for the book.

In New York at the Uris Theatre for previews in February, after more than six weeks in Detroit, *Seesaw* finally clicked in the second week, suddenly coming alive as a cohesive, exuberant show that audiences related to—just in time for its new opening date of March 18. Except that Kasha and Kipness, who'd spent a million dollars so far, including the new sets that cost $100,000 and new costumes for $80,000, had no money left. That's when the personnel involved started taking salary cuts and royalty deferments. Bennett paid the Nederlanders, who ran the Uris Theatre, $15,000 of his own money so the show could open on a Sunday night instead of the scheduled Saturday, because that way, no matter what happened with the critics, the producers would

SEESAW (DETROIT)

SYNPOSIS OF SCENES

The action of the Play takes place in New York City
in the course of a year.

ACT II

1. ROOSEVELT HOSPITAL
"Visitors" . . . . .Hospital Staff

"We've Got It" . . . . .Jerry

2. ON THE WAY HOME
"Poor Everybody Else" . . . . .Gittel

3. GITTEL'S APARTMENT
Reprise: "We've Got It" . . . . .Jerry, Gittel

4. LYCEUM THEATRE
"Ride Out the Storm" . . . . .Sophie

5. THE LOFT
"Chapter 54, Number 1909" . . . . .Larry, Gittel and Tap Class

Reprise: "Poor Everybody Else" . . . . .Gittel and Full Company

6. JERRY'S APARTMENT
7. 1665 BROADWAY
"Megatron" .Gittel, Larry and Dance Company

"It's Not Where You Start" . . . . .Larry, Gittel, Sophie,
Ralph, Gretchen and Hardhats

8. JERRY'S APARTMENT, GITTEL'S APARTMENT
9. WASHINGTON SQUARE PARK
Reprise: "Seesaw" . . . . .Ralph, Gretchen and Morning People

10. PRINCE ST. SUBWAY STATION
Reprise: "It's Not Where You Start" . . . . .Sophie, Gittel

11. JERRY'S APARTMENT, GITTEL'S APARTMENT
Reprise: "More People Like You" . . . . .Jerry

"I'm Way Ahead" . . . . .Gittel

SEESAW (NEW YORK)

SYNPOSIS OF SCENES

The action of the Play takes place in New York City

PROLOGUE

"Seesaw" . . . . .Full Company

TIMES SQUARE AREA

"My City" . . . . .Jerry Ryan and the Neighborhood Girls

DANCE STUDIO ON WEST 54TH STREET

"Nobody Does It Like Me" . . . . .Gittel

JAPANESE RESTRAURANT ON 46TH STREET AND LINCOLN CENTER

"In Tune" . . . . .Gittel and Jerry

EAST 116TH STREET

"Spanglish" . . . . .Julio Gonzales, Gittel, Jerry,
Sophie and Full Company

GITTEL'S APARTMENT IN THE EAST VILLAGE

"Welcome to Holiday Inn!" . . . . .Gittel

JERRY'S APARTMENT

"You're a Lovable Lunatic" . . . . .Jerry

GITTEL'S APARTMENT, THEN THE STREET

"He's Good for Me" . . . . .Gittel

THE BANANA CLUB

"Ride Out the Storm" . . . . .Sparkle, Sophie and Full Company

GITTEL'S APARTMENT

ACT II

ST. VINCENT'S HOSPITAL

"We've Got It" . . . . .Jerry

"Poor Everybody Else" . . . . .Gittel

DANCE STUDIO

"Chapter 54, Number 1909" . . . . .David, Jerry,
Gittel and Dance Company

JERRY'S APARTMENT
BACKSTAGE AT THE THEATRE

"The Concert" . . . . .Gittel and Dance Company

"It's Not Where You Start" . . . . .David and Full Company

CENTRAL PARK, LATER THAT NIGHT
GITTEL'S APARTMENT, PHONE BOOTH AT KENNEDY AIRPORT
GITTEL'S APARTMENT, 2:00 a.m.
GITTLE'S APARTMENT, JERRY'S APARTMENT, A FEW DAYS LATER

"I'm Way Ahead"

"Seesaw" (reprise) . . . . .Gittel

have to pay the cast the week's wages, and therefore the show would at least run a week.

Seesaw did open on Sunday, March 19, to standing ovations and solid reviews, some glowing, and all indications were for a solid run. But the next day the producers were forced to put up the closing notice backstage, because there was no money to run the show past the following Saturday—eight performances away. Then Dorothy put in $30,000 of her own money so the closing notice could come down. Everyone rallied to dredge up $6,000 to use Rex Reed's rave review on a radio spot. Earl Wilson gave the show a plug every day in his *New York Post* column. The company, led by Tommy Tune, performed numbers from the show on the street outside the theatre while stagehands and musicians passed out flyers to passersby. Then in a publicity coup, Ethel Watt, the wife of *Daily News* critic Douglas Watt, asked Mayor John Lindsay (who looked uncannily like leading man Ken Howard) to appear onstage, which he did on Friday night, during the opening number, "My City." Not only did the audience go wild, but every television news camera in New York was present backstage; the stagehands waived the $3,000 fee to which they were entitled in the event of anyone being photographed inside the theatre. Business picked up from a disastrous $17,539 in the last week of previews (the break-even weekly figure was $60,000) to $55,241 by the first week of performances and $60,794 in the second week (business on the morning after the mayor's visit alone was worth some $21,000). Finally, there were lines at the box office and *Seesaw* built an advance.

Everyone involved felt they'd been through a profound experience, having pulled together and put their egos and individual interests aside, simply because nobody could stand to see this show they believed in die. Dorothy felt the exhilaration of the team effort. But at age sixty-eight, surrounded by virtually all "kids," she also came out of the *Seesaw* experience with a deep weariness about the state of Broadway and its future. Publicly, anyway, she was determined to think positively. "It's impossible to do a Broadway show

WHEN SEESAW FINALLY SETTLED INTO A BROADWAY RUN

after its tumultuous beginnings, arrangements got under way for a national tour. Auditions were held for the lead role of Gittel. Lucie Arnaz was one of the performers who showed up for the audition.

"I was studying with the coach David Craig, and David knew Dorothy Fields well. He always told everybody that when you're auditioning for songwriters, you never sing their songs for the audition. But he said this would be the exception—he wanted me to sing 'Look Who's in Love' from *Redhead*. Also, he'd always said, 'Never change lyrics,' but he said, 'Here are some special lyrics that are very Gittel. Tell Dorothy Fields that David Craig suggested it.' So I went to the audition, and I sang 'Look Who's in Love' with the special lyrics. And when I was through, nobody said anything. And I looked out into the blackened theatre, and I put my hand up against the light so I could see where Dorothy Fields was sitting. And I called out, 'Miss Fields?' And this voice came back, 'Yes . . .' And I started to explain how I changed the lyric, and said, 'David Craig said you wouldn't mind.' And there was this silence, and after a minute all I heard, in this voice that sounded like Tallulah Bankhead underwater, was, 'Did he. . . .'"

Arnaz got the part.

New York City mayor John Lindsay makes a guest appearance in *Seesaw*, 1973

NOBODY DOES IT LIKE ME

If there's a wrong way to say it,
A wrong way to play it,
Nobody does it like me.
If there's a wrong way to do it,
A right way to screw it up,
Nobody does it like me.

I've got a big loud mouth,
I'm always talking much too free.
If you go for tact and manners,
Better stay away from me.
If there's a wrong way to keep it
   cool,
A right way to be a fool,
Nobody does it like me.

If there's wrong bell I ring it,
A wrong note I sing it,
Nobody does it like me.
If there's a problem I duck it,
I don't solve it, I just muck it up,
Nobody does it like me.

And so I try to be a lady
I'm no lady, I'm a fraud,
And when I talk like a lady
What I sound like is a broad.
If there's a wrong way to get a
   guy,
A right way to lose a guy,
Nobody does it like me.

SEESAW (DETROIT)

CAST

IN ORDER OF APPEARANCE

Ralph . . . . .Richard Ryder

Gretchen . . . . .Chris Wilzak

Gittel Mosca . . . . .Lainie Kazan

Jerry Ryan . . . . .Ken Howard

Landlord . . . . .Stanley Simmonds

Boy in Phone Booth . . . . .Felix Greco

Girl in Phone Booth . . . . .Merel Poloway

Larry . . . . .Bill Starr

Oscar . . . . .Lou Genevrino

Counterman in Deli . . . . .Don Swanson

Juilo Rodriguez . . . . .Giancarlo Esposito

Mrs. Rodriguez . . . . .Gloria Irizarry

Armando Rodriguez . . . . .Burt Rodriguez

Chico Rodriguez . . . . .Felix Greco

Lolita Rodriguez . . . . .Loida Iglesias

Subway Riders . . . . .John Almberg, Charles Rule,
Stanley Simmonds, Clyde Walker

Phone Repairman . . . . .Wayne Cilento

Sophie . . . . .Joshie Jo Armstead

Girl in Organic Restaurant . . . . .Bonnie Brody

Laertes . . . . .Felix Greco

Hamlet . . . . .Burt Rodriguez

Osric . . . . .Lou Genevrino

Queen Gertrude . . . . .Yolanda Raven

King Claudius . . . . .Bobby Johnson

Horatio . . . . .Clyde Walker

Fortinbras . . . . .William Swiggard

Soldier . . . . .Steve Anthony

Soldier . . . . .Michael Reed

Dentist . . . . .Jay Fox

Frank Taubman . . . . .Charles Rule

Anne Taubman . . . . .Bonnie Walker

Girl at Party . . . . .Jean Even

Intern . . . . .Orrin Reiley

Doctor . . . . .Terry Deck

Attendant . . . . .Jay Fox

Nurse . . . . .Cathy Brewer-Moore

Nurse's Aide . . . . .Judy Gibson

Woman-in-Traction . . . . .Mitzi Hamilton

Director . . . . .Orrin Reiley

Stage Manager . . . . .William Swiggard

Miss Hudson . . . . .Dona D. Vaughn

Miss Cartwright . . . . .Eileen Casey

Tess Ryan . . . . .Amanda McBroom

Theatre Patron . . . . .Charles Rule

His Wife . . . . .Michon Peacock

Hardhats . . . . .John Almberg, Charles Rule,
Stanley Simmonds, Clyde Walker

First Bus Driver . . . . .Charles Rule

Second Bus Driver . . . . .Stanley Simmonds

Norma . . . . .Michon Peacock

Augie . . . . .Judy Gibson

Swing Girl . . . . .Stephanie Lynne

Swing Boy . . . . .Jerry Yoder

SEESAW (NEW YORK)

CAST

(IN ORDER OF APPEARANCE)

Jerry Ryan .... Ken Howard

Gittel Mosca .... Michele Lee

David .... Tommy Tune

Sophie .... Cecelia Norfleet

Julio Gonzales .... Giancarlo Esposito

Sparkle .... LaMonté Peterson

Nurse .... Judy McCauley

Ethel .... Cathy Brewer-Moore

---

CITIZENS OF NEW YORK

John Almberg, Steve Anthony, Cathy Brewer-Moore, Eileen Casey,
Wayne Cilento, Patti D'Beck, Terry Deck, Judy Gibson, Felix Greco,
Mitzi Hamilton, Loida Iglesias, Bobby Johnson, Baayork Lee,
Amanda McBroom, Judy McCauley, Anita Morris, Gerry O'Hara,
Michon Peacock, Frank Pietri, Yolanda Raven, Michael Reed,
Orrin Reiley, Don Swanson, William Swiggard, Tom Urich,
Dona D. Vaughn, Thomas J. Walsh, Chris Wilzak.

Swings—Jerry Yoder, Merel Poloway.

today," she told Rex Reed in an interview following the popular conclusion that *Seesaw* had become a sleeper hit, "but you do it anyway, for love."

The score, which was not the tour de force that *Sweet Charity* had been, nevertheless yielded her most mature and skilled soloquizing, as in "I'm Way Ahead." Other songs, particularly "Nobody Does It Like Me" and "It's Not Where You Start, It's Where You Finish," went on quickly to become standards. *Seesaw* finished out the year, running just over nine months, enough to have wedged itself firmly in Broadway annals.

The following March, exactly a year after the heroic Broadway launch, rehearsals began for the national company, headed by Lucie Arnaz. On Thursday, the 28th, Dorothy left rehearsals at the end of the afternoon and returned to her apartment in the Beresford to rest and get ready to show up for a fund-raiser headed by Burton Lane. Shortly after she arrived home, without any warning, she suffered a fatal stroke. It was three months before her sixty-ninth birthday.

Dorothy's death was widely mourned at all levels of the music and theatre communities. Stanley Adams, president of ASCAP, pronounced her "the most important woman writer in the history of ASCAP." Her children chose items from her collection and gave something she liked to each of her close friends as a keepsake.

In the business her parents had tried so hard to keep her out of, Dorothy had written nineteen Broadway musicals, lyrics for over thirty movies, and totaled close to five hundred songs. Though her career met the occasional requisite misfire, it was a career marked by extraordinarily consistent success, leading her once to quip in true Fields style, "If, God forbid, we ever had a flop, I'd go to Sardi's and cut my throat, quietly, with a grapefruit knife." In the years before her death, she had been honored and feted many times, not only with her charter induction into the otherwise all male Songwriters Hall of Fame, but at a benefit evening for the Theatre Collection of the Museum of the City of New York. Another such occasion was a night honoring her work, with Dorothy speaking and singing onstage, at the venerable Lyrics and Lyricists series

THE NIGHT DOROTHY DIED, SHE WAS SUPPOSED

to appear at a benefit hosted by Burton Lane. Lane, whose daughter was mentally handicapped, was raising funds for the Young Adult Institute, and had secured Sheldon Harnick, Yip Harburg, and Cy Coleman to entertain for the evening, along with Dorothy. When the news about why Dorothy hadn't shown up was phoned to Lane, he, along with the rest of the theatre community, was stunned. Lane, who had first met her in the 1920s when he was a teenager starting out in the business, delivered one of the eulogies at her memorial service, in which he said, "How does one define generosity when it relates to Dorothy? If one were to call Santa Claus generous, he is generous only once a year. But Dorothy was Santa Claus all year around."

POOR EVERYBODY ELSE

Poor everybody else
How I pity everybody else but me.
I'm sorry they're not loved like I'm being loved.
In this world there's no girl alive got the goosebumps that I've got.

Today, feel so rich today
I'd give everything but him away.
This town would flip but they just can't make the contact
He's under exclusive contract to me.
Poor everybody else, pity everybody else
I could sit down and cry for poor everybody else but me.

Poor everybody else
My heart aches for you and you and you and
  you.
We're physically tied, spiritually tied.
Like he says, we're interdependers like pants
  and suspenders.

We match, crazy how we match
And what's more we hit it off from scratch.
I love my friends, but just in case they are
  tempted
Remember the guy's pre-empted by me.
Poor everybody else, lonely everybody else
Got a lump in my throat for poor everybody
  else but me.

at the 92nd Street Y (the same place where Charity and Oscar were trapped in the elevator).

There, shortly before *Seesaw* was to go into rehearsals, she gave the SRO crowd her doctrine: "Sounds and rhyming can be beguiling only when they state exactly what you should say. Don't fall in love with what you believe is a clever rhyme, it can throw you. Think about what you want to say and then look for the most amusing or graceful way you can say it."

As if to prove her point, she ended her fifty-year career as a wordsmith with the indelibly straightforward declaration:

> It's not where you start, it's where you finish.
> It's not how you go, it's how you land.
> A hundred-to-one shot, they call him a klutz,
> Can outrun the favorite, all he needs is the guts.
>
> Your final return will not diminish
> And you can be the cream of the crop.
> It's not where you start, it's where you finish
> And you're gonna finish on top.

EPILOGUE

A FEW YEARS AFTER HER DEATH and the agonies of putting *Seesaw* onstage, Dorothy Fields made an unexpected return to Broadway. With the nostalgia craze in full swing, *Sugar Babies* arrived at the Mark Hellinger Theatre in 1979, produced by Harry Rigby, who had also produced the nostalgia-kick revivals of *Irene* and *No, No, Nanette*. *Sugar Babies* was a burlesque extravaganza with songs and sketches not far from the music hall variety shows Lew Fields perfected in his heyday (including a dog act, a juggler, and a tribute to fan dancer Sally Rand). Wildly successful (and the first hit revue in many years), it starred veterans Mickey Rooney and Ann Miller. But the score belonged to Dorothy Fields and her first partner, Jimmy McHugh. Fifty years after they'd introduced their songs to a world that had yet to see the Great Depression or World War II, a new generation of audiences was captivated. Once again it was possible to leave a Broadway theatre singing "Don't Blame Me," "I Can't Give You Anything but Love," and "On the Sunny Side of the Street."

SONG LIST

Contributed by Ken Bloom

All lyrics by Dorothy Fields unless otherwise indicated.

DATE UNKNOWN

POP SONGS: Moody's Mood (C McHugh, Jimmy)

1926

POP SONGS: I'm a Broken Hearted Blackbird (C McHugh, Jimmy)

1928

POP SONGS: Bon Soir Cherie (C McHugh, Jimmy); Harlem River Quiver (C McHugh, Jimmy); Collegiana (C McHugh, Jimmy)

SHOW AND FILM SONGS

Lew Leslie's Blackbirds of 1928 (Show). Music by Jimmy McHugh: Baby!* Bandanna Babies*Diga Diga Doo*Dixie*Doin' the New Low-Down*Here Comes My Blackbird*I Can't Give You Anything but Love*I Must Have that Man*Magnolia's Wedding Day*Porgy (Blues for Porgy)*Shuffle Your Feet (and Just Roll Along)

Hello Daddy (Show). Music by Jimmy McHugh: As Long as We're in Love* Futuristic Rhythm*I Want Plenty of You*In a Great Big Way*Let's Sit and Talk about You*Maybe Means Yes*Out Where the Blues Begin*Party Line* Three Little Maids from School*Your Disposition Is Mine

1929

POP SONGS: For One Another (C McHugh, Jimmy); Hot Chocolate (C McHugh, Jimmy); Hottentot Tot (C McHugh, Jimmy); A Japanese Dream (C McHugh, Jimmy); A Japanese Moon (C McHugh, Jimmy); Let Me Sing Before Breakfast (C McHugh, Jimmy); Think of You Think of Me in the Moonlight (C McHugh, Jimmy)

SHOW AND FILM SONGS

Cotton Club Parade (Nightclub). Music by Jimmy McHugh: Arabian Lover* Freeze an' Melt*Hot Feet

The Time, the Place and the Girl(Film). Collegiana (C McHugh, Jimmy)

Ziegfeld Midnight Frolic (Show). Music by Jimmy McHugh: Looking for Love* Squeaky Shoes*What a Whale of a Difference Just a Few Lights Make

Ziegfeld Midnight Frolic (2d 1929 edition) (Show). Music by Jimmy McHugh: Because I Love Nice Things*I Can't Wait*Raisin' the Roof

1930

POP SONGS: Dance Fool, Dance (C McHugh, Jimmy); Rosalie (C McHugh, Jimmy); Spring Fever (C McHugh, Jimmy); Topsy and Eva (C McHugh, Jimmy)

SHOW AND FILM SONGS

The International Revue (Show). Music by Jimmy McHugh: Big Papoose Is on the Loose*Cinderella Brown*Exactly Like You*Gypsy Love*I Could Go for You*I'm Feelin' Blue 'Cause I've Got Nobody (cut)*International Rhythm*I've Got a Bug in My Head*I've Got the Blues*Keys to Your Heart*Make Up Your Mind*The Margineers*On the Sunny Side of the Street*Spain*That's Why We're Dancing

Kelly's Vacation (Unknown). Music by Jimmy McHugh: Man on Earth Is Worth Half a Dozen on the Moon; Any One Else*Do I Know Why*Dreaming*Wearin' of the Green

Love in the Rough (Film). Music by Jimmy McHugh: Go Home and Tell Your Mother*I'm Doin' that Thing*I'm Learning a Lot from You*Like Kelly Can*One More Waltz

March of Time (Film). There's a Kick in the Old Girl Yet (C McHugh, Jimmy)

A Social Success (Film). Isn't Nature Wonderful (C McHugh, Jimmy)

The Vanderbilt Revue (Show). Music by Jimmy McHugh: Blue Again*Button Up Your Heart*Cut In*You're the Better Half of Me

1931

POP SONGS: Cheerio (C McHugh, Jimmy; Stothart, Herbert); Harlemania (C McHugh, Jimmy); I'm So Backward and She's So Forward) (C McHugh, Jimmy); It Costs Nothing to Dream (C McHugh, Jimmy); Lolita (C McHugh, Jimmy); Love Magician (C McHugh, Jimmy); Nobody's Fool (C McHugh, Jimmy); Scene on the Dock (C McHugh, Jimmy; Stothart, Herbert); There's Love in the Air (C McHugh, Jimmy)

SHOW AND FILM SONGS

Cuban Love Song (Film). Music by Jimmy McHugh and Herbert Stothart: Cuban Love Song*Tramps at Sea

Flying High (Film). Music by Jimmy McHugh: Examination Number*I'll Make a Happy Landing (the Lucky Day I Land You)*We'll Dance Until the Dawn

Rhapsody in Black (Show). I'm Feelin' Blue (C McHugh, Jimmy)

Shoot the Works (Show). How's Your Uncle? (C McHugh, Jimmy)

Singin' the Blues (Show). Music by Jimmy McHugh: It's the Darndest Thing*Singin' the Blues

1932

POP SONGS: Ain't It the Truth (C McHugh, Jimmy); Happy Times (C McHugh, Jimmy); I've Got a Date with Kate (C McHugh, Jimmy); Then You Went and Changed Your Mind (C McHugh, Jimmy); Whisper in the Moonlight (C McHugh, Jimmy)

SHOW AND FILM SONGS

Dancers in the Dark (Film): It's the Darndest Thing (C McHugh, Jimmy)

Radio City Music Hall Opening (Show). Music by Jimmy McHugh: Happy Times*Hey Young Fella! (Close Your Old Umbrella)*Journey's End*With a Feather in Your Cap

1933

POP SONGS: Dinner at Eight (C McHugh, Jimmy); I've Got a Roof over My Head (C McHugh, Jimmy); In the Little White Church on the Hill (C McHugh, Jimmy); Let's Sit This One Out (C McHugh, Jimmy); Let's Whistle a Waltz (C McHugh, Jimmy); Pride of the Mountainside (C McHugh, Jimmy); What Is There About You? (C McHugh, Jimmy)

SHOW AND FILM SONGS

Clowns in Clover (Show). Music by Jimmy McHugh: At Sea*Clowns in Clover* Don't Blame Me*Hey Young Fella (Close Your Old Umbrella)*I'm Full of the Devil*Make Up Your Mind*The Margineers (also in **The International Revue**)*My Favorite Person*Play Half a Chorus*Positively Love You* Prologue

Dancing Lady (Film). My Dancing Lady (C McHugh, Jimmy)

Meet the Baron (Film). Music by Jimmy McHugh: Bus Ride Sequence*Clean as a Whistle*Dinner at Eight*Don't Blame Me*Drumming Out*Hail to the Baron Munchausen*Musical Opening

The Prize Fighter and the Lady (Film). Lucky Fella (C McHugh, Jimmy)

1934

POP SONGS: Debutante (C McHugh, Jimmy); Dinah's Daughter (C McHugh, Jimmy); El Choclo (C/L: Fields, Dorothy; McHugh, Jimmy; Villoldo, A.P.); I Love Cardenias (C McHugh, Jimmy); Lucky Duck (C McHugh, Jimmy); Moonlight on the Riviera (C McHugh, Jimmy); Over on the Jersey Side (C McHugh, Jimmy); Say How D'Ye Do-a to Kalua (C McHugh, Jimmy); Serenade for a Wealthy Widow (C/L: Fields, Dorothy; Forsythe, Reginald, McHugh, Jimmy); Sing You a Couple of Choruses (C McHugh, Jimmy); Step In (C McHugh, Jimmy); Tell Me (C McHugh, Jimmy); Who Said that Dreams Don't Come True (C McHugh, Jimmy)

SHOW AND FILM SONGS

Fugitive Lovers (Film). Full of the Devil (C McHugh, Jimmy)

Have a Heart (Film). Music by Jimmy McHugh: Lost in a Fog*Thank You for a Lovely Evening

Strictly Dynamite (Film). Goodbye Blues (C/L: Fields, Dorothy; Johnson, Arnold; McHugh, Jimmy)

1935

POP SONGS: Every Little Moment (C McHugh, Jimmy); Harlem at Its Best (C McHugh, Jimmy)

SHOW AND FILM SONGS

Alice Adams (Film), I Can't Waltz Alone (C Steiner, Max)

Every Night at Eight (Film). Music by Jimmy McHugh: Every Night at Eight*I Feel a Song Comin' On (L: Fields, Dorothy; Oppenheimer, George)*I'm in the Mood for Love*It's Great to Be in Love Again*Speaking Confidentially*Take It Easy*That's the Hollywood Low-Down

Hooray for Love (Film). Music by Jimmy McHugh: Hooray for Love*I'm Livin' in a Great Big Way*I'm in Love All Over Again*Palsie Walsie*You're an Angel

I Dream Too Much (Film). Music by Jerome Kern: I Dream Too Much*I Got Love*I'm the Echo (You're the Song I Sing)*The Jockey on the Carousel

In Person (Film). Music by Oscar Levant: Don't Mention Love to Me*Got a New Lease on Life*Out of Sight, Out of My Mind

The Nitwits (Film): Music in My Heart (C McHugh, Jimmy)

Roberta (Film). Music by Jerome Kern: Fashion Show*I Won't Dance (L: Fields, Dorothy; Hammerstein II, Oscar)*Lovely to Look At*Russian Lullaby

1936

SHOW AND FILM SONGS

The King Steps Out (Film). Music by Fritz Kreisler: Learn How to Lose*Madly in Love*Stars in My Eyes*What Shall Remain?

Swing Time (Film). Music by Jerome Kern: Bojangles of Harlem*A Fine Romance*It's Not in the Cards*Never Gonna Dance*Pick Yourself Up*Swing Low, Swing High*The Way You Look Tonight

1937

SHOW AND FILM SONGS

When You're in Love (Film). Music by Jerome Kern: Our Song*The Whistling Boy

1938

SHOW AND FILM SONGS

The Joy of Living (Film). Music by Jerome Kern: Heavenly Party*Just Let Me Look at You*What's Good about Good-Night?*You Couldn't Be Cuter

1939

SHOW AND FILM SONGS

Stars in Your Eyes (Show). Music by Arthur Schwartz: (He's) Goin' Home*All the Time; As of Today; I'll Pay the Check; It's All Yours; Just a Little Bit More*A Lady Needs a Change*Never a Dull Moment; Okay for Sound*One Brief Moment*Places, Everybody; Self-Made Man*Terribly Attractive*This Is It

Sticks and Stones (Show). Swing Left, Sweet Chariot (C Henderson, Ray)

1940

SHOW AND FILM SONGS

One Night in the Tropics (Film). Music by Jerome Kern: Back in My Shell*Farandola*Remind Me*You and Your Kiss

1945

POP SONGS: Let's Have an Old-Fashioned Christmas (and Pray for a Happy New Year) (C Adamson, Harold); Sergeant Housewife (C Meyer, Joseph)

SONG LIST

SHOW AND FILM SONGS

Up in Central Park (Show). Music by Sigmund Romberg: April Snow*The Big Back Yard*The Birds and the Bees*Boss Tweed*Carousel in the Park*Close as Pages in a Book*Currier and Ives*The Fireman's Bride*It Doesn't Cost You Anything to Dream*Opening Scene III*Opening Scene V*Rip Van Winkle*Up from the Gutter*When She Walks in the Room*When the Party Gives a Party*You Can't Get Over the Wall

1948

SHOW AND FILM SONGS

Up in Central Park (Film): Oh! Say Can You See (C Romberg, Sigmund)

1950

SHOW AND FILM SONGS

Arms and the Girl (Show). Music by Morton Gould: A Cow and a Plough and a Frau*Don't Talk*A Girl with a Flame*He Will Tonight*I Like It Here*I'll Never Learn*I'll Never See You Again (cut)*I'm Scared*Johnny Cake*Little Old Cabin Door*Mister Washington! Uncle George!*Nothin' for Nothin'*Plantation in Philadelphia*She's Exciting*That's My Fella*That's What I Told Him Last Night*There Must Be Somethin' Better than Love*You Kissed Me

1951

SHOW AND FILM SONGS

Excuse My Dust (Film). Music by Arthur Schwartz: Get a Horse*Goin' Steady*I'd Like to Take You Out Dreaming*It Couldn't Happen to Two Nicer People*Lorelei Brown*One More You*Spring Has Sprung*That's for Children*Where Can I Run from You

Mr. Imperium (Film). Music by Harold Arlen: Andiamo*Let Me Look at You*My Love an' My Mule

Texas Carnival (Film). Music by Harry Warren: Carnie's Pitch*It's Dynamite*Love Is a Lovely Word*Schnapps*Whoa, Emma*You've Got a Face Full of Wonderful Things*Young Folks Should Get Married

A Tree Grows in Brooklyn (Show). Music by Arthur Schwartz: The Bride Wore Something Old (cut)*Call on Your Neighbor*Don't Be Afraid*Growing Pains*He Had Refinement*I'll Buy You a Star*I'm Like a New Broom*If You Haven't Got a Sweetheart*Is That My Prince?*Look Who's Dancing*Love Is the Reason*Make the Man Love Me*Mine 'til Monday*Oysters in July (cut)*Payday*That's How It Goes*Tuscaloosa (cut)

1952

SHOW AND FILM SONGS

The Big Song and Dance (Film). Music by Arthur Schwartz: Boys Are Better than Girls*Dance Me Around*Goin' with the Birds*I Did It and I'm Glad*I'm Proud of You*Now Is Wonderful*The Profezzor*Where Do I Go from You

Lovely to Look At (Film). Music by Jerome Kern: I'll Be Hard to Handle (L: Dougall, Bernard; Fields, Dorothy)*Lafayette*The Most Exciting Night*Opening Night*When We Were Very Young (Terzettino)*You're Devastating (L: Fields, Dorothy; Harbach, Otto)

1953

SHOW AND FILM SONGS

The Farmer Takes a Wife (Film). Music by Harold Arlen: Can You Spell Sche-
nectady?*The Evils of Drink!*Happy the Bride the Sun Shines Upon*I
Could Cook*I Was Wearin' Horseshoes*Look Who's Been Dreaming*On the
Erie Canal*Opening; Somethin' Real Special*Today I Love Everybody*
We're Doin' It for the Natives in Jamaica*We're in Business*When I Close
My Door*Why Am I Happy?*With the Sun Warm Upon Me*Yes!

1954

POP SONGS: It Not Where You Start (C Schwartz, Arthur)

SHOW AND FILM SONGS

By the Beautiful Sea (Show). Music by Arthur Schwartz: Alone Too Long*Coney
Island Boat*Good Time Charlie*Hang Up!*Happy Habit*Hooray for George
the Third*I'd Rather Wake Up by Myself*It's All Mine (cut)*It's Not Where
You Start (cut)*It's Up to You (cut)*Lottie Gibson Specialty (Please Don't Send
Me Down a Baby Brother)*Me and Pollyanna (cut)*Moments from Shake-
speare (cut)*Mona from Arizona*More Love than Your Love*Old Enough to
Love*The Sea Song (By the Beautiful Sea)*Thirty Weeks of Heaven (cut)*
Throw the Anchor Away*Tuscaloosa (cut)

1956

POP SONGS: April Fooled Me (C Kern, Jerome); Introduce Me (C Kern,
Jerome); Nice to Be Near (C Kern, Jerome)

1957

POP SONGS: Marcha Del Toros (C Kern, Jerome)

SHOW AND FILM SONGS

Junior Miss (TV Musical). Music by Burton Lane: The Happy Heart*Have Feet
Will Dance*I'll Buy It*It's Just What I Wanted*Junior Miss*Let's Make It
Christmas All Year Long*A Male Is an Animal

1959

SHOW AND FILM SONGS

Redhead (Show). Music by Albert Hague: Behave Yourself*Dream Dance*'Erbie
Fitch's Twitch*I'll Try*I'm Back in Circulation*It Doesn't Take a Minute
(cut)*Just for Once*Look Who's in Love*Merely Marvelous*My Gal's a Mule
(cut)*My Girl Is Just Enough Woman for Me*The Right Finger of Me Left
Hand*She's Not Enough Woman for Me*The Simpson Sisters*Two Faces in
the Dark*The Uncle Sam Rag*We Loves Ya, Jimey

1966

SHOW AND FILM SONGS

Sweet Charity (Show). Music by Cy Coleman: Baby, Dream Your Dream*Big Spender*Charity's Soliloquy*Did You Ever Look at You (cut prior to opening)*Free Thought in Action Class Song (cut prior to opening)*Gimme a Raincheck (cut prior to opening)*A Good Impression (cut prior to opening)*I Can't Let You Down (cut prior to opening)*I Love to Cry at Weddings*I'll Take Any Man (cut prior to opening)*I'm Way Ahead (cut prior to opening)*I'm a Brass Band*I'm the Bravest Individual*I've Tried Everything (cut prior to opening)*If My Friends Could See Me Now*Keep It in the Family (cut prior to opening)*Pink Taffeta Sample Size 10 (cut prior to opening); Poor Everybody Else (cut prior to opening)*The Rhythm of Life*Sweet Charity* There's Gotta Be Something Better than This*Too Many Tomorrows*When Did You Know? (cut prior to opening)*Where Am I Going?*You Can't Lose 'em All (cut prior to opening)*You Should See Yourself*You Wanna Bet (cut prior to opening)

1968

SHOW AND FILM SONGS

The Hell with Heroes (Film): Where There Is Love (C Jones, Quincy)

Sweet Charity (Film). Music by Cy Coleman: It's a Nice Face*My Personal Property*Sweet Charity

1969

POP SONGS: Five O'Clock Sky (C Lahm, David); Where There Is Love There Is Hope (C Jones, Quincy)

1970

SHOW AND FILM SONGS

Eleanor (Show) (unproduced). Music by Cy Coleman: After Forty It's Patch, Patch, Patch*Charge*A Good Impression*I Can't Let You Go*I Struck Out* Keep It in the Family*Love and Logic*Meat and Potatoes*The Old Kitchen Sink*Red Hot Tomatoes*Sixty Percent of the Accidents*So What Now?* What Do I Do?*When Did You Know*Whisper on the Wind

1973

SHOW AND FILM SONGS

Seesaw (Show). Music by Cy Coleman: Big Fat Heart (cut)*Chapter 54, Number 1909; Did You Ever Look at You (cut)*He's Good for Me*Hospitality (cut)* I'm Way Ahead*I'm in a Highly Emotional State*In Tune*It's Not Where You Start*More People Like You (cut)*My City*Nobody Does It Like Me*The Party's on Me (added for tours)*Pick Up the Pieces (cut)*Poor Everybody Else*Ride Out the Storm*Salt (cut)*Seesaw (1) (cut)*Seesaw (2)*Spanglish* Tutu and Tights (cut)*Visitors (cut)*We've Got It*Welcome to Holiday Inn* You're a Lovable Lunatic

INDEX OF TITLES

Boldface page numbers represent photographs.

GENERAL INDEX

"I Feel a Song Comin' On," music by Jimmy McHugh. Robbins Music Corp., 1935. Reprinted by permission. All rights reserved.

"Lovely to Look At," music by Jerome Kern. T. B. Harms Co, 1935. Reprinted by permission. All rights reserved.

"I Won't Dance," music by Jerome Kern, lyrics by Dorothy Fields, Otto Harbach, Jimmy McHugh, Oscar Hammerstein II. Reprinted by permission. All rights reserved.

"I Dream Too Much," music by Jerome Kern. T. B. Harms Co, 1935. Reprinted by permission. All rights reserved.

"A Fine Romance," music by Jerome Kern. T. B. Harms Co., 1936. Reprinted by permission. All rights reserved.

"Never Gonna Dance," music by Jerome Kern. Reprinted by permission. All rights reserved.

"Pick Yourself Up," music by Jerome Kern. Reprinted by permission. All rights reserved.

"The Way You Look Tonight," music by Jerome Kern. Reprinted by permission. All rights reserved.

"You Couldn't Be Cuter," music by Jerome Kern. T. B. Harms Co., 1938. Reprinted by permission. All rights reserved.

"A Lady Needs a Change," music by Arthur Schwartz. Chappell & Co., Inc., 1939. Reprinted by permission. All rights reserved.

"Remind Me," music by Jerome Kern. Chappell & Co., Inc., 1940. Reprinted by permission. All rights reserved.

"Close as Pages in a Book," music by Sigmund Romberg. Williamson Music, Inc., 1944. Reprinted by permission. All rights reserved.

"Nothin' for Nothin'," music by Morton Gould. Chappell & Co., Inc., 1950. Reprinted by permission. All rights reserved.

"There Must Be Something Better Than Love," music by Morton Gould. Chappell & Co., Inc., 1950. Reprinted by permission. All rights reserved.

"A Cow and a Plough and a Frau," music by Morton Gould. Chappell & Co., Inc., 1950. Reprinted by permission. All rights reserved.

"He Had Refinement," music by Arthur Schwartz. Putnam Music, Inc., 1951. Reprinted by permission. All rights reserved.

"Make the Man Love Me," music by Arthur Schwartz. Putnam Music, Inc., 1951. Reprinted by permission. All rights reserved.

"I'll Buy It," music by Burton Lane. Chappell & Co., Inc., 1957. Reprinted by permission. All rights reserved.

"'Erbie Fitch's Twitch," music by Albert Hague. Chappell & Co., Inc., 1958. Reprinted by permission. All rights reserved.

"Big Spender," music by Cy Coleman. Notable Music, Inc., 1965, Reprinted by permission. All rights reserved.

"I Love to Cry at Weddings," music by Cy Coleman. Notable Music, Inc., 1965. Reprinted by permission. All rights reserved.

"If My Friends Could See Me Now," music by Cy Coleman. Notable Music, Inc., 1965. Reprinted by permission. All rights reserved.

"I'm a Brass Band," music by Cy Coleman. Notable Music, Inc., 1965. Reprinted by permission. All rights reserved.

"Pink Taffeta Sample Size 10," music by Cy Coleman. Notable Music, Inc., 1965. Reprinted by permission. All rights reserved.

"Where Am I Going?," music by Cy Coleman. Notable Music, Inc., 1965. Reprinted by permission. All rights reserved.

"You Should See Yourself," music by Cy Coleman. Notable Music, Inc., 1965. Reprinted by permission. All rights reserved.

"It's Not Where You Start, It's Where You Finish," music by Cy Coleman. Notable Music, Inc., 1972. Reprinted by permission. All rights reserved.

"Nobody Does It Like Me," music by Cy Coleman. Notable Music, Inc., 1973. Reprinted by permission. All rights reserved.

"Poor Everybody Else," music by Cy Coleman. Notable Music Co., 1972. Reprinted by permission. All rights reserved.

PHOTO CREDITS

Courtesy of Mary Cleere Haran: pp. 4, 7 (l.), 12, 15, 105, 108, 182

Courtesy of Eliza Lahm Brewster: pp. 7 (r.), 118

Courtesy of David Lahm: pp. 10, 19, 74, 243

Billy Rose Theatre Collection: The New York Public Library for the Performing Arts, Astor, Lenox and Tilden Foundations: pp. 23, 51, 57 (White Studio), 59, 75, 77, 78,80, 85, 87, 111, 112, 113, 125 (Vandamm), 130 (Vandamm), 131 (Vandamm), 134, 138, 143, 148 (Vandamm), 151, 152, 155, 158, 163 (Freidman-Abeles), 164 (Vandamm), 169, 170, 177 (Friedman-Abeles), 183, 184, 185, 186, 187 (Vandamm), 191, 192 (Vandamm), 197, 202, 215, 223, 225, 229, 237

Courtesy of Frank Wiener: pp. 25, 28, 39, 60, 64, 66, 67, 71, 93, 195

Bettman Archive: pp. 29, 103, 209

Courtesy of Lucille Meyers: pp. 31, 33, 55, 69

Author's collection: p. 139